Pathways to School Success

Leaving No Child Behind

Norris Haynes

UNIVERSITY PRESS OF AMERICA,® INC.
Lanham • Boulder • New York • Toronto • Oxford

Copyright © 2006 by
University Press of America,® Inc.
4501 Forbes Boulevard
Suite 200
Lanham, Maryland 20706
UPA Acquisitions Department (301) 459-3366

PO Box 317
Oxford
OX2 9RU, UK

Library of Congress Control Number: 2006922977
ISBN-13: 978-0-7618-3408-3 (paperback : alk. ppr.)
ISBN-10: 0-7618-3408-7 (paperback : alk. ppr.)

I dedicate this book to my children and
to all the children of the world.

Contents

Foreword

In the United States of America, the achievement gap between students of different socio-economic and ethnic backgrounds remains wide and continues to be a major source of concern. National Assessment of Educational Progress (NAEP) scores on reading in 2000 indicated that only 32 percent of fourth graders could read at a proficient level thereby showing academic success. Also, whereas scores for the highest performing students have improved over time, those for many of America's lowest performing students have declined (NAEP, 2001). This achievement gap persists and many children are still being left behind despite the fact that the federal government has spent more than $242 billion through between 1965 when the Elementary and Secondary Education Act (ESEA) was passed and 2003, to help educate children from poor backgrounds.

The good news is that some schools in cities and towns across the nation are helping children who have traditionally experienced low performance begin to experience academic success. If some schools can succeed in helping all children achieve school success, then all schools should be able to help the lowest achieving child achieve academic success.

The No Child Left Behind (NCLB) Act passed by Congress in 2001 is designed to enhance the culture and climate of American schools and to increase the numbers of children from every segment of society achieve school success. NCLB is built on four principles or pillars:

- Accountability for results
- Emphasis on teaching methods and programs that are based on strong scientific research and evidence

- Expanded options for parents and parent involvement in school improvement
- Expanded local control and flexibility

Pathways to School Success: Leaving No Child Behind is intended to encourage constructive conversation and suggest practical approaches to enhancing children's learning and achievement in schools while in the process, fulfilling the underlying premise of the No Child left Behind Act, that no child, rich or poor, should be left behind. The purpose of this book is not to argue pro or con about the merits of NCLB and the extent to which the mandates of NCLB can be met with the level of funding available to meet those mandates. The purpose for writing this book is to illuminate the essence of effective teaching and learning in schools and to underscore the need for student-centered approaches to schooling. It is written for individuals whose goal is to make a positive difference in children's lives through responsible and responsive schooling practices that will lead to school success.

The pathways described in this book are premised on the developmental work that the author has done throughout his professional career including his work with Dr James Comer on the developmental pathways. The author briefly revisits the six developmental pathways in Chapter one as a backdrop to considering the seven pathways to success that he proffers in this book. An understanding of Child development and its role in fostering and nurturing school success is a critical undergirding element in promoting effective teaching and learning in schools.

The seven pathways to school success that the author presents in this book are different from developmental pathways in their concreteness and specificity. The six developmental pathways offer a global framework for understanding the importance of supporting the development of the whole child. The seven pathways to school success are designed to deepen the knowledge and understanding of those who are engaged in educating children, of the multifaceted elements in schooling practices that help children to succeed, thereby reducing the probability of leaving any one child behind.

Vygotsky's notion of the Zone of Proximal Development (ZPD) this author believes, is a time-tested truth, that children do bring to the educational arena unique skills and talents and potentialities for success that can and should be developed. Children need caring, supportive, dedicated adults to help mold and fashion those potentialities into successful behaviors and strategies. Classroom teachers, and helping professionals such as social workers, school counselors, school psychologists, special education teachers and speech therapists all bring to the educational enterprise specialized skills that can collectively make learning a positive and pleasant experience for all children.

The role that parents can and should play in helping their children achieve school success cannot be overstated. Parent involvement takes different forms and occurs in a variety of ways. Many models of parent involvement exist all with varying degrees of success. While parental involvement is not presented as a distinct success pathway in this book, it is acknowledged as a key factor in students' success that should permeate every facet of the students' educational experiences. It is an important and irreplaceable cornerstone of student success.

Chapter One

Multiple Pathways to School Success

Educators and other school-based professionals have unique opportunities to address children's physical, social, emotional and academic development. However, for the past several decades, despite many years of innovative school reform initiatives, school success for many children remains an elusive dream. Many children continue to lag far behind expected levels of achievement (Chubb, John E. & Loveless, Tom, 2002) and many still continue to drop out of school. (Balfanz & Legters, 2004)

Dryfoos (1994) summarized the challenge that American schools faced then and continue to face today. She noted:

> "American schools are failing because they cannot meet the complex needs of today's students. Teachers cannot teach hungry children or cope with young people who are too distraught to learn. Anyone working in an inner-city school, in a marginal rural area, or even on the fringes of suburbia will tell you how impossible her or his job has become. The cumulative effects of poverty have created social environments that challenge educators, community leaders, and practitioners of health and, mental health, and social services to invent new kinds of institutional responses." (p. xv)

The work of non-teaching school-based professionals should not be seen to be divorced from the school's primary focus of educating and preparing children well to be productive members of our society. School- based support professionals can intervene in ways that strengthen the school's role in promoting, supporting and sustaining children's overall development, and helping them to be educated well enough to preserve and sustain physically, socially and emotionally healthy lives while achieving significant academic success. Indeed, it is evident that children who demonstrate proficiency in social and academic areas of their lives also tend to be among the most academically successful. (Zins, Weissberg, Wang, Walberg, 2004).

Like good social and emotional development, healthy physical development is also important and indeed essential to school success. Dr. Louis Sullivan (1992), the former Secretary of Health and Human Services, made the observation that: "good health is essential to children's growth and development, to their ability to take advantage of educational opportunities, and to their future prospects. Children and adolescents must be healthy in order to learn, and they must learn in order to be healthy" (p. 1).

THE EVOLVING ROLE OF SCHOOLS

Schooling has evolved over the past decades from simply socially engineering children into specific jobs and trades based on the pre-assessed societal needs, (scientific management orientation) to highly personalized and child-centered educational approaches designed to meet the developmental needs of the whole child. The following considerations are now driving educational reform with implications for school health promotion:

1. What do children need in order to develop well and succeed in school and in life?
2. How is each child different and how does this uniqueness influence what and how he/she learns?
3. How can all of the adult stakeholders in the school, work with families and community agencies and service providers, to provide support for children and the best opportunities for them to learn and lead healthy lives?
4. How can the school serve as the pivotal center of service delivery and access to address the multiple and interrelated physical, mental health, educational and psychosocial needs of children and families?

Comer, Haynes, Joyner and Ben-Avie (1996) advanced a theory of developmental pathways along which children must experience optimum development in order to be well adjusted, healthy and successful in school and in life. The pathways are:

Physical: this pathway is concerned with promoting the physical health of children. It includes good nutritional education and programs, physical health education and activities, and access to health and dental care education and services. within this pathway we also ensure that children's vision and hearing are checked as regularly as needed to ensure that they can see to read and hear well enough to learn and understand subject matter content.

Language: this pathway is concerned with helping children develop appropriate written and spoken language skills. An essential aspect of children being healthy and maintaining their good physical and psychological health is the ability to articulate one's needs, express one's points of view and engage in meaningful and constructive conversation with others. Success in school and in life to a very large extent depends on one's ability to communicate effectively through the written and spoken word.

Ethical: this pathway is concerned with helping children develop good decision making skills. This involves helping them learn to make good judgments, especially in problem situations, and to make choices that are healthy and positive. Making wise choices in school and outside of school can make the difference between success and failure, health and illness, life and death. We must give children the skills to analyze and assess choice alternatives and decide on the best and most healthy choices. Good development along this pathway reduces the occurrence of high risk behaviors such as: alcohol and drug abuse, promiscuous and unprotected sexual activity which leads to early and unplanned pregnancies, and sexually transmitted diseases and AIDS, and reckless disregard for the rights of others.

Social: this pathway is concerned with promoting children's ability to interact socially with other children and with the significant adults in their lives. It has to do with what Howard Gardner calls "interpersonal intelligence". The ability to problem solve in social situations and to negotiate constructively leading to win situations, reduces the incidence of violence in our schools and communities and makes young people and all of us much safer and more secure.

Psychological: this pathway is concerned with the intra-psychic well-being of children; their self-esteem and self-evaluations of their worth and value as individuals in school and outside of school. We must provide children in schools with experiences that lead to enhanced self-worth, self-efficacy and well-being. We must also attend to the increasing incidence of depression and anxiety, and to the devastating impact of Post Traumatic Stress Disorder (PTSD) resulting from exposure to violence, on children's psychological and emotional health.

Cognitive: this pathway is concerned with providing children with the knowledge and skills that would enable them to think critically, and to be creative. We must help children in schools acquire effective problem solving skills and the ability to apply concepts of learning in a variety of contexts. When children develop well cognitively, they are likely to succeed in school and to lead productive and healthy lives as adults.

Schools help children to develop well along these six pathways by fostering collaboration between parents and staff, among school-based health and mental health providers, and by connecting health care providers and services to schools and to one another. It is important for schools to take a developmentally informed approach to promoting children's overall heath. Efforts must begin very early in children's lives to have maximum benefit. The results from long-term evaluative studies on early interventions indicate that if interventions are implemented early and effectively in helping to promote, preserve and protect children's health there can be long-term educational and social benefits for these children (Consortium for Longitudinal Studies, 1983; Lazar, Darlington, Murray, Royce, & Snipper, 1982; Campbell & Ramey, 1995; Ramey & Campbell, 1991; Currie and Thomas, 1995; Currie and Thomas, 1997).

LINKAGES BETWEEN SCHOOL PROMOTION OF PHYISICAL, SOCIAL AND EMOTIONAL HEALTH AND STUDENT SUCCESS

Researchers have documented the significant effects of school health-promoting climate and programs on children's health and academic outcomes. Lisbeth Schorr (1988) cited many studies which showed that "rotten outcomes such as teen pregnancy and adolescent fatherhood, school failure are the results of poverty, poor choices and generally inadequate development along the pathways that Comer theorized about. Millstein, Petersen, and Nightingale (1993), discussed evidence linking high-risk behaviors among adolescents such as promiscuous sexual activity, teen pregnancy, violence, drug abuse and alcoholism, not only with poverty and social class, but also with school learning and school success, relationships with adults and peer-group relationships. They also reported on successful interventions which address not just the symptoms of troubled youth but the root causes in systematic ways. Dryfoos (1994) provided a comprehensive report on how schools were being transformed into comprehensive service delivery centers for children and families and the positive impact this had on children's health and achievement.

HOW CAN PHYSICAL, SOCIAL AND EMOTIONAL HEALTH PROMOTION IN SCHOOLS BE BEST PROMOTED AND SUPPORTED

Teaching and non-teaching school-based professionals can make significant contributions to children's overall physical, social and emotional health in schools in a number of important ways:

1. be more proactive and preventive in our work. Providing treatment and cure for children's physical, psychological and emotional illnesses is very important. But far too often our work is reactive and curative and sufficiently preventative.
2. begin to see our work in more developmental terms, identifying the critical social and psychological factors and challenges which children are facing at different points in their lives and structure our intervention strategies to be sensitive and responsive to these factors as much as possible.
3. work in greater collaboration with our colleagues in specialties other than our own who are involved in providing services to schools where we work or who serve the same individual children that we serve.
4. connect our interventions to the goals of the school and also help to inform the goals and programs of the school. In other words, we can be seen as advocates and active participants in promoting the health of children in the school in ways that complement and inform the school's efforts.
5. use collective knowledge, skill and influence to connect schools with needed services that exist outside of the school to help increase access to important and vital services to children and families.
6. continually evaluate our work with regard to the goals set forth for children and for schools. The extent to which we collectively and individually achieve or do not achieve these goals can be informative to us as we seek to be the best, and most effective health and mental health providers for children in our schools.
7. use individual and collective power to influence legislation, policies and practices that impact our ability to serve children and schools well, recognizing that sometimes school district, state and national policies can limit our work on behalf of children in our schools.

It is often said that our children are the country's and the world's best, most promising and greatest resource. If this is true, then school success—producing strategies can and must promote, support and sustain children's overall healthy development. It is for this reason that the role of schools is so crucial and school physical, social and emotional health promotion is so vital. It is important to ensure that children in schools are as physically, socially and emotionally healthy as possible, so that they can learn well and become successful, well-adjusted adults and be responsible, productive members of our society.

In the chapters that follow, the author outlines and discusses social and emotional pathways to school success drawing upon the important lessons learned from many years of work in helping to implement and assess work related to the implementation of programs designed to address the developmental pathways outlined above. The social and emotional pathways to school success in clude the following:

- Responsive Schools
- School-Based Support Services
- Personalized Learning Communities
- Students' Interest, Achievement and Motivation
- Positive School Climate Factors
- Fostered Resilience
- School Readiness

REFERENCES

Balfanz, R & Legters N (2004). Locating the dropout crisis. Center for Social Organization of Schools. Johns Hopkins University.

Campbell, F. A., & Ramey, C. T. (1995). Cognitive and school outcomes for high-risk African American students at middle adolescence: Positive effects of early intervention. *American Education Research Journal*, 743–772.

Chubb, J. E. & Loveless, T. (Eds.). (2002). *Bridging the Achievement Gap*. Washington, D.C: Brookings Institution Press.

Comer J. P., Haynes, N. M., Joyner, E. & Ben-Avie M. (1996) *Rallying the whole village: The Comer Process for reforming education*. New York: Teachers College Press.

Consortium for Longitudinal Studies (1983). *As the twig is bent: Lasting effects of preschool programs*. Hillsdale, NJ: Erlbaum.

Currie, J., & Thomas, D. (1995). Does Head Start make a difference? *The American Economic Review*, 341–364.

Currie, J. M., & Thomas, D. (1997; April). Does subsequent school quality explain differential effects of Head Start? In W. S. Barnett (Chair), *Early preschool, medical, and family support services for families with young children: What makes a difference?* Symposium conducted at the biennial meeting of the Society for Research in Child Development, Washington, DC.

Dryfoos, J. S. (1994). Full-service schools*: A revolution in health and social services for children, youth and families*. San Francisco: Jossey–Bass

Lazar, I., Darlington, R., Murray, H., Royce, J., & Snipper, A. (1982). Lasting effects of early education: A report from the Consortium for Longitudinal Studies. *Monographs of the* Society for Research in Child Development, 47(2–3, Serial No. 195).

Millstein, S. G., Petersen, A. C. & Nightingale, E. O. (eds.) (1993). *Promoting the health of adolescents*. New York: Oxford University Press.

Schorr, L. B. (1988). *Within our reach: Breaking the cycle of disadvantage*. New York: Anchor Press.

Sullivan, L. (1992). Foreword to: Healthy Schools: A Directory of Federal Programs and Activities Related to Health Promotion Through The Schools. Washington, DC: U.S. Department of Health and Human Services.

Zins, J., Weissberg, R. P., Wang, M. C. & Walberg, H. J. (2004). Building success on social and emotional learning: What does the research say? New York: Teachers College Press.

Chapter Two

Pathway One: Responsive Schools: Acceptance, *B*elief and *C*hallenge

For school experiences to be worthwhile and for children to succeed, schools need to be responsive to their needs. Responsive schools demonstrate what this author calls the ABC of educational responsibility: *A*cceptance, *B*elief, and *C*hallenge. (Haynes, 1993)

Low academic achievement is often viewed from a purely cognitive perspective as evidence of low academic ability, or from a socio-cultural perspective as the internalization of value systems that impede intellectual development. However, The complex social and emotional factors, including interpersonal interactions within schools that influence students achievement cannot be ignored.(Zins, Bloodworth, Weissberg, Walberg, 2004) Among these interactions is the nature and level of acceptance that students experience, the belief and expectations that teachers hold for students, and the ways in which students are challenged in schools and classrooms. Schools that promote positive self-esteem, confidence and high self-expectations among students are more likely to produce academic success and positive personal growth compared to schools that do not expect and support high achievement.

School staff demonstrate acceptance of all children by respecting their individuality and differences, and demonstrate their belief in their potential for success by maintaining high performance standards and by motivating them through highly stimulating pedagogical approaches that respond to their unique learning styles. Acceptance involves the provision of opportunities in schools for the expression of culture, for the exchange of cultural information in an atmosphere of mutual respect, and for individual growth. The school's curriculum, text books, social agenda, student population, teachers, staff human interactions and evaluation practices reflect the acceptance level of the school. When children from different backgrounds and experiences feel equally comfortable and respected in a school, then the acceptance level in that school is high.

Belief in students' potential to succeed and do well is an important factor in their school performance. The literature confirms that the fact expectancy effects are still very much alive in schools and classrooms. Expectancy effects often lead to self-fulfilling prophecies in which beliefs about students affect the way they are taught, and because the teaching is premised on beliefs about some students' academic abilities, these students respond in ways that confirm these beliefs. Some educators believe that many students come from dysfunctional backgrounds and that these students themselves are intrinsically and inherently deficient in intellectual skills and cannot learn. When educators believe that some students cannot learn or do not want to learn and that their presence in a classroom or school is disruptive, and an impediment to the learning of others, policies and procedures are adopted which disadvantage these children. Serious efforts to effect positive change and growth among low-achieving students recognize that the argument of inherent intellectual superiority or inferiority is a false argument, that social conditions do not have to be a limiting factor because strategies can be implemented to change conditions and that social status does not have to limit academic ability.

Many students come from severely stressful social conditions. Their existence is often marginal to the mainstream of American society and they often see little hope for a bright future. Despite the social isolation and economic deprivation faced by many of these children, they often come to schools with as much potential, eagerness to learn, and willingness to please adults as other children. They are no less intelligent, no less capable, and no less malleable then their more privileged counterparts. The problem very often is that these students, fueled in part by messages they receive from others may perceive themselves as being less able than they are.

Children from very poor backgrounds can, and do succeed when school environments are responsive to their needs. Effective schooling must address students' academic, social and emotional needs by providing qualitatively relevant and meaningful curricula and adequate contextual supports for all them. The socially and emotionally responsive learning environment practices good ABC (Acceptance, Belief and Challenge) and has a school climate, supported by an educational philosophy, that fosters respect and caring

To effectively challenge students by meeting their social and emotional needs schools should:

1. be sensitive and responsive to students' socio-cultural needs.
2. include relevant examples from a variety of socio-cultural backgrounds in teaching and learning activities.

3. create a climate that provides acceptance and positive belief.
4. set high standards of performance.
5. reward achievement and address deficits.
6. provide hope for a better life.
7. help students set and achieve reachable goals.
8. engage the interest and involvement of parents.
9. have fair and helpful assessment techniques.
10. provide adequate resources to support development and learning.

REFERENCES

Haynes N. (1993). Critical issues in educating African-American children. Langley Park: IAAS Publishers.

Zins, J., Bloodworth, M. R., Weissberg, R. P. & Walberg, H. J. (2004). The scientific base linking social and emotional learning to school success. In J, Zins, R. Weissberg, M. Wang & H. Walberg (eds.) Building success on social and emotional learning: What does the research say? New York: Teachers College Press.

Chapter Three

Pathway Two:
School-Based Support Services

A steady increase in social and related problems has had a negative impact on students' ability to complete school successfully. Changes in family structure, poverty, and economic instability are just a few of the challenges which both weaken a family's capacity to care for children and limit their ability to access assistance. Children are therefore bringing problems with them to school that interfere with learning (Romualdi & Sandoval, 1995). By the fourth grade, the academic performance of most American children is below minimum achievement standards: 75% of students are not proficient in reading, 66% are not proficient in writing, and 82% do not meet appropriate math levels. School failure in turn contributes to the rising social problems. According to Comer & Haynes (1995), early school failure is a major predictor of later school, work, and life failure or difficulty, as well as of more severe mental health problems.

There is a definite association among mental health status, psychological conflict, social problems and educational achievement (Dryfoos, 1993; Comer & Haynes, 1995). Social crises, like homelessness, exposure to violence and drugs, and inadequate adult supervision, contribute to the onset of diagnosable mental health conditions and behavior difficulties (Wagner, 1994). The serious impact of these pressures on children's development is evident in the increasing numbers of school-aged children in need of psychological/psychiatric intervention for stress induced symptoms such as: depression, hyperactivity and attention deficit disorders, oppositional behaviors, externalizing and conduct disorders, and substance abuse delinquency (Comer & Haynes, 1995). In fact, one out of five youth aged 10 to 18 suffer from a diagnosable mental disorder, and one out of four report symptoms of emotional disorders (Dryfoos, 1993). Children under more psychosocial pressure fare worse in school. Many high risk students are children with either identified or unidentified behavioral and emotional problems. For example, in Maine 10% of school dropouts have been identified as having a disorder, and 66% have an unaddressed behavioral or emotional problem Children's mental health disorders, including emotional and behavioral problems have a large social, psychological, cultural, and economic impact on families and communities(Osher & Hanley, 1996). Although the problems most visibly and directly affect families with school-aged children, the problem is not limited to them. Society as a whole is paying a price for not intervening in this cycle of social problems that lead to behavioral or emotional difficulties, which in turn lead to school failure, and begin the cycle again. Corporations, for example, are spending $210 billion annually on formal and informal training of poorly educated employees (Peeks, 1993). Hence, the public is essentially financing education twice: once with tax dollars—public and private spending on education is $189 billion (Peeks, 1993)—and again when corporations increase product costs in order to pay for necessary training. Primary prevention and early intervention are clearly much more cost effective than paying for the consequences of not intervening.

Changes in social, economic, family, and demographic factors demand public schools to do more, yet school standards and services have not changed much in the last 25 years (Carnegie, 1996), so students are unprepared to meet today's challenges. There has been some effort to address children's social issues and the array of mental health problems which they cause or maintain (Wagner, 1994). Unfortunately, the increase in services has not kept pace with the increase in social stress factors; therefore, the need for services continues to exceed the available resources (Comer & Haynes, 1995).

Although the primary mission of an educational system is academic development, if they are to accomplish educational goals schools need to assume more responsibility for addressing these social and behavioral issues: "Where underdevelopment or bad development has taken place [in a child] prior to school, schools must support adequate development of experience failure [in the promotion of development along cognitive/academic pathways]" (Comer & Haynes, 1995, p. 3). Most literature supports this contention that social competence and psychological well-being are significantly related to academic achievement; students can learn to the full extent of their abilities if they are under less psychological duress (Boger, 1990; Peeks, 1993).

Schools should address students' total development by integrating the input and expertise of significant adults in children's lives. Schools are optimal service delivery sites because of the number of students and families they have the potential to reach. Children are mandated to attend school, and school is really the only common setting remaining for children (Talley &

Short, 1996; Dryfoos, 1993; Comer & Haynes, 1996b). This factor helps conquer barriers to service delivery such as time and transportation (Osher & Hanley, 1996), as well as giving care workers access to high-risk, needy populations who would not ordinarily receive services (Dryfoos, 1993). The benefits of this approach extend beyond the immediate care received; they also teach students and families why and how to access services in the future (Dryfoos, 1993).

Schools are also very influential on children's growth because of the amount of time children spend in school. At least half of a child's developmental period is spent in school (Osher & Hanley, 1996; Educators need to assume responsibility for the developmental environment that they have direct control over, namely the school setting. School is the first opportunity professionals have to reinforce positive growth and development began in the community and family or to compensate for underdevelopment (Comer & Haynes, 1995) This is important because primary care takers are either failing to recognize treatable problems or are unable to handle them (Zahner, PAwelkiewicz, DeFrancesco & Adnopoz, 1992)

The school's period of influence coincides with children's most important developmental period. This makes the school's role even more important. The long-term success of learning and development largely depends on what happens to a child between the ages of three and ten (Carnegie, 1996). During this period, it is especially important that children establish a high level of attachment that enables adults to influence their behavior (Comer & Haynes, 1996b). As school demands exceed preparation, and cognitive capacity increases to allow an understanding of social problems, the ability of adults to influence positively children's behavior and aspirations decreases when the child is around nine years old, if he/she is without attachments (Comer & Haynes, 1996b).

Although schools can have a positive influence on children, they can also have a negative impact if they do not take their responsibility seriously. A child's mental health condition can become aggravated both by interactions in school and by the schooling process. School-related stress plays a role in triggering predisposed conditions; the potential for conflict and for psychological stress is high in schools for staff, students, and parents because of the many people involved in the educational process and because of different goals, motivations, and backgrounds of people within the school (Comer & Haynes, 1995). Hence, differences in educational performance are not the result of differences in students' inherent ability to learn. These differences are a culmination of the failure of schools to respond to increasing needs of students who are under more social pressure; their low expectations; a heavy reliance on ineffective curricula and teaching methods; poorly prepared, insufficiently supported teams; weak home-school linkages; a lack of accountability systems; and poor resource allocation (Carnegie, 1996).

Educators realize that children are failing, but reform mechanisms have mainly focused on increasing excellence through competency tests and cognitive skills work; (Purkey & Aspy, 1988). This strategy does not help students, especially those at high risk, unless it is accompanied by strong support services (Knitzer et al, 1991). This emphasis on increasing test scores has caused a neglect of affective education and developmental concerns that affect student growth (Purkey & Aspy, 1988). Reform efforts will be costly and ineffective as long as their underlying developmental and social issues remaining unaddressed. Despite this fact, neither federal nor local school reform policies have encouraged changes in the educational process that will support the overall development of students and address increasing social challenges How should schools address the social problems and psychological stress kids are grappling with? The ecological/systems approach to school reform is the most effective way to support whole child development and to make long-lasting improvements in children's lives. The best way to understand a school and the people within in it is to look at its organizational culture—the guiding beliefs and expectations for how a school operates and how people relate to each other (Thacker, 1994). Most problem and solutions stem from the ecological or systems level, not the individual level; therefore, it is at the systems level where intervention is most effective. Ehly (1993) summarizes the critical assumptions behind the ecological change model: (1) children are considered to be inseparable parts of the targeted social system, (2) disturbance is assumed to reflect the system rather than a disease of problems located within the child; the environment can be structured to influence behaviors, and (3) problems are cast as a failure of match between the child and the system; both the abilities of the child and the expectations of the system need to be in line with one another. The end result of the ecological approach as applied to school reform is a successful child centered whole school change.

Mental health and support service providers, such as psychologists and social workers, make optimal school change agents within the ecological approach because their professional training gives them the background and skills to implement the child-centered reform processes previously discussed. In order for any system changes to be effective, individuals who have expertise in planning, problem solving, and facilitating organizational change need to be involved in the planning and implementation of changes (Curtis & Stollar, 1996). Psychologists and other support service providers are in the best position to fulfill this need for experts. They should have the skills to be able to sustain broad reform goals while still remaining within their field of expertise, as they target cognitive, affective, and structural components of the school system (Curtis & Stollar, 1996). If the reform goals are student centered as they should be, schools need to rely on the competencies of counselors regardless of who is implementing the changes. Ysseldyke and Geenen (1996) cite particular competencies that could be used by counselors. Included are collaborative skills; communication, conflict management, and problem solving skills; individual and group counseling skills; consulting skills; diagnostic testing skills; and knowledge about child development and social issues.

In order to deliver services in schools effectively, counselors and psychologists need to be comfortable navigating throughout the various systems in which children interact, e.g. family, peer, school, and community systems (Conoley & Conoley, 1991). To act as a school reform facilitator would not require a significant role change for support service providers, it would simply involve applying their work and theoretical orientation to the whole school. Given the connection that exists between behavior, emotion, and learning (Talley & Short, 1996), schools should benefit from applying knowledge of psychology at the community, school, classroom, and individual levels (Riley, 1996). For example, Comer & Haynes (1996b) identified several issues that emerge in school which require knowledge of behavioral and social sciences that psychologists and other support service providers have: school size and architecture, compensatory education programs, issues related to busing and school desegregation, management of trauma, racial identification issues, class and race relations, and gender issues. Other roles have been identified for support service providers to complement their function as behavior and development experts. Behavioral scientists, for example, can promote health-enhancing behavior to prevent many health disorders (Thomas, 1987) and address health disorders that have psychological or environmental roots, e.g. eating disorders (Talley & Short, 1996).

Using their already developed professional skills, support service providers could help students balance academic, social, emotional, and behavioral demands (Riley, 1996) while reducing psychosocial dynamics that interfere with learning (Comer & Haynes, 1995). On another level, psychologists and social workers can also provide support to teachers. Service professionals can be used as consultants to help teachers solve problems before they escalate (Riley, 1996); they are crucial agents in structuring, delivering, and evaluating interventions at the classroom level (Ehly, 1993). In particular they can teach school staff: (a) how student fears and anxieties influence behavior, (b) how excessive control and punishment worsens behavior, (c) how motivation grows out of the affective component of learning, (d) how staff behaviors dictate student responses, (e) how child development and social conditions factor into learning (Comer & Haynes, 1996b; Comer & Haynes, 1995). Increasing staff and parent understanding of development and behavior through consultation will improve student behavior and academic performance.

Mental health workers and other support service professionals are currently not being used to their full capabilities. Most continue to follow the tradition of providing adjunct services, marginal to the daily functioning of the school The current, unenlightened system only provides students and families with the necessary attention and access to resources after a problem has escalated out of control (Elias, 1995; Romualdi & Sandoval, 1995). If counselors are going to be of help to educators and students, they need to increase access to both crisis intervention and case management services that are connected to the school life of the child.

Increasingly, the bulk of support service professionals' time has been spent on special education-related tasks. School systems are mandated to provide appropriate educational programs, assessment, and evaluation for special needs children (Thomas, 1987). The unintended result of this federal mandate was a reduction in regular services and attention for the general school population, and a heavy focus on testing and assessment of children with learning, behavioral, or emotional problems.

The role of psychologists in implementation of this act was designed to include assessment and evaluation, consultation, psychological counseling, and parent training, but theory has not manifested itself in practice (Dwyer & Gorin, 1996). There is a significant discrepancy between the role stated by school counselors as ideal and the actual role being fulfilled. Ideally, counselors would like to emphasize classroom guidance; parent and faculty workshops; and consulting (Carroll, 1993), but most do not have the time to assume any additional responsibilities. Some school psychologists are participating in Goals 2000, the federal education goals, by assisting with violence prevention programs (Goal 7), improving curriculum and instruction (Goals 3 & 5), and promoting home-school collaboration (Goal 8) (Ysseldyke & Geenen, 1996). These are positive steps, but support personnel are still not being assigned an active role in the school reform process because they are too busy serving a select portion of the school population.

The service delivery system has remained crisis oriented and reactive partially because providers are overwhelmed with demands for services. Fifteen to 19% of US children need mental health care (Wagner, 1994), but at current staffing levels support cannot be provided for all students. Even of those students in most serious need of counseling, only 25–40% are receiving assistance amounting to approximately 22.8 hours per year for each child (Osher & Hanley, 1996). A 1988 national education longitudinal study found that only 11% of eighth graders had had the opportunity to speak to a school counselor or teacher about a personal problem within the last year (Dryfoos, 1993). Empirical research has recommended a caseload of 300 students per school counselor (Carroll, 1993), yet Dryfoos (1993) found that there are approximately 70,000 guidance counselors in public schools which averages to about 1 counselor per 600 children. One person could certainly not provide adequate individual support for 600 people.

The federal government is not supporting increased support services either (Dryfoos, 1993; Knitzer et al, 1991), which exacerbates the marginalization of these important mental health and social services within a school. At the state level, only eleven states have legislation mandating elementary school counseling. The result is that there are too few support service professionals working in schools to meet demands for health, psychological, and social services (Ehly, 1993), let alone enough to have a lasting impact on the school as a whole (Osher & Hanley, 1996). Fifty-eight percent of schools have no capacity to provide any counseling services.

Support personnel are among the first to be eliminated in budget cuts (Dryfoos, 1993; Adelman, 1996); clearly administrators and communities do not recognize their importance. This is in part because few educators include addressing social problems among the school's responsibilities (Ehly, 1993), or consider themselves complex social systems (Comer & Haynes, 1995). This has led to a clear separation between education and mental health within the minds of educators. According to Comer & Haynes (1995), this separation is evident at the national, state, and local levels: first, in the lack of cooperation between the National Institute of Mental Health and the National Institute of Education; second, in the lack of cooperation between state departments of education and mental health in service delivery and research; third, in the minimal consultation services and cooperation between mental health workers and educators.

Support service providers are also partially to blame for their insignificant role in the educational system. There is a lack of understanding of the counselor's role within the school, so counselors should do more to define and explain their position (Bailey, Deery, Gehrke & Perry, 1989). Role expectations do vary from district to district depending on needs of the school (Thomas, Orf, Levinson & Pinciotti, 1992. However, there is still too much role confusion which decreases support for the counselor's services. The general school population is not sure why the psychologist works in a certain way, how the approach meets the needs and goals of the school, how decisions are made, and what arrangements exist to maintain accountability (Comer & Haynes, 1995).

Other problems with the delivery system include fragmented and uncoordinated services. Because school service professionals often operate in isolation from each other, they frequently engage in a duplication of efforts or conflicting interventions (Adelman, 1993; Romualdi & Sandoval, 1995). Programs have failed to coordinate services within the school and community and the students have paid the price with inefficient and costly services, as well as a lack of continuity in programming for various problems and across grade levels (Elias, 1995; Adelman, 1993). In one New York school where there were 200 different prevention and treatment programs operating concurrently, even the principal could not identify the function of any of the programs (Dryfoos, 1993). It is less effective to divide problems into strict categories because children often have multiple, interconnected needs (Osher & Hanley, 1996). This concept is not understood by the decision makers, most of whom do not have a counseling background—yet another reason for increasing the role support service providers play in schools. It is interesting to note that school service use statistics contradict the lack of importance placed on school based support services. A study by Zahner et. al. (1992) found that in a population of children aged 6–11 years old, 28.3 % of the total sample had service contact and 51.2% of the at risk students had access to services. The overall service use of the sample was considerably larger than estimates for the general child population of 5% and 10–20% respectively (Zahner et. al., 1992). School service usage accounted for the difference. When service usage was restricted to other settings, the rates of service were comparable to national levels (Zahner et. al., 1992).

Despite the shortcomings of the current school service system, when programs are well implemented, funded, and staffed they can be quite effective because of the large numbers of students and families who opt for school services when they are available. Given the extensive use of school mental health and social support services, more importance should be placed on providing adequate services for children within the school setting, and on the role of the support service professionals who work within a school.

Researchers have identified several areas where school support service professional could expand their influence while using a systems approach and focusing on the whole child. Social reform in education that emphasizes educational achievement, whole-child development, and school climate offers great potential for enhancing the role of the school support staff such as psychologists and social workers. The common denominator of all such reform proposals is collaboration. Multidisciplinary teams composed of counselors, administrators, psychologists, teachers, social workers, and parents are widely supported, especially when the model has the mental health professional acting as the case manager. While the psychologist, for example, would coordinate the group effort, it is important that the input and concerns of each team member carry equal weight. Each team member brings a different perspective to education and this cooperative forum allows them to maximize their individual contributions by making interventions consistent and comprehensive (Thomas, 1987). Such a team meets the requirements for an effective school reform agent; it would enhance classroom based efforts to enable learning, provide assistance to students and families, prevent crises, support transitions, increase home involvement in schooling, and develop greater community involvement and support (Adelman, 1996).

In districts where a large number of students are underdeveloped, the inevitable high levels of conflict and tension can be reduced by having collaborative management teams that involve administrators, teachers, parents, mental health professionals, and students (Comer & Haynes, 1995). A sample of the characteristics of this team approach which make it effective for improving student outcomes includes: collaborative planning, ownership by the school, the role of the principal, the use of a case manager, shared resources, and staff development (Dolan, 1992).

Evidence exists that the case management team approach, under the direction of support service professionals, reduces fragmentation and redundancy of services, increases treatment acceptability, increases generalization of treatment gains, and increases the school's success in managing behavior and learning environments (Conoley & Conoley, 1991). Service delivery also becomes more outcome oriented, consumer driven, and cost conscious (Romualdi & Sandoval, 1995; Shawl, Kelly Joost & Parker-Fisher 1995), as well as less intimidating and easier to access (Dawling & Taylor, 1989).

The team approach should reduce individuals' respective case loads allowing the professional to dedicate more time and expertise to the school population as a whole. The benefits of this extra time are seen in a team approach advocated by O'Dell et al (1996), which combines (a) developmental programming aimed at improving the personal, social, and goal planning competencies of all students, (b) preventive programming which targets at-risk students, and (c) remedial programming which serves troubled students. The effects of the program on the school included positive changes in self-concept, a lower failure rate, realistic career planning, higher school functioning, and increased understanding. Clearly, the case management team approach has the greatest impact when there is a commitment to whole-child/whole-school problem solving and an equal focus on individual assessment and systemic issues (Romualdi & Sandoval, 1995; Talley & Short, 1996).

True collaboration also facilitates the development of shared ownership for goal setting and achievement, effective communication, mutual respect, and open-mindedness (Vesey, 1996). Confidence and farifiliarity with the mental health professional then opens the door for successful consultation at program and organizational levels (Abec, 1987). This level of consultation and collaboration is necessary for systemic change; all major stakeholders must be committed (Curtis & Stollar, 1996). Although systemic change is the end goal, it is important that the team processes be integrated into already existing mechanisms within the school or community; this approach will facilitate a smooth transition, and prohibit cutting back on existing resources (Dryfoos, 1993; Adelman, 1996).

Coordinated services naturally follow from collaboration, since teams will find that no single resource can provide all the services children will need to develop well (Haynes & Comer, 1996). Some schools are now offering children and families a range of services that are centralized under an umbrella organization based either in the school or the community. It is frequently recommended that, in order to satisfy students' diverse needs sufficiently, a comprehensive services network, i.e. including mental health, medical, and social services, needs to be standard for all schools (Dryfoos, 1993). Interdisciplinary service coordination broadens the focus of services, stresses collaboration between many social settings which affect kids, and changes the school's climate (Clancy, 1995). Services should not be limited to mandated services such as special education, but should address the specific needs of a community as determined by the support services team (Romualdi & Sandoval, 1995). All people involved would be part of the decision-making structure.

Several schools have recognized the benefits of physician-psychologist/ counselor collaboration because of the reciprocal link among education, social issues, and health. These schools are now successfully applying this model in order to expand their school-based clinics (Talley & Short, 1996; Shaw et al, 1995; Dryfoos, 1993). Talley & Short (1996) found that a truly comprehensive services program must include sequential services in eight different areas: health education, physical education, health services, nutrition services, health promotion, counseling/ psychological/ social services, a healthy school environment, and parent/ community involvement. The expanded role for support service workers would include participation in implementation and administration of services; direct and indirect service provision; interfacing of health and educational outcomes; and research and evaluation (Tharinger, 1995). According to Haynes & Comer (1996), the entire community benefits from an integrated services approach. Students receive expanded learning opportunities, the attention of caring adults, and increased motivation to stay in school. Families get increased access to social services and an increased ability to network with child development experts and other parents. The school gets a network of services from which to draw support for learning processes.

There is a clear need for integration of support services professionals into schools.(Dolan, 1992). Many programs around the country serve as examples of promising school-based programs which are rising to meet the multiple needs of children in order to improve student school adjustment and success. In order to educate effectively, schools need to address each developmental pathway affecting children's learning capabilities. Mental health workers, including school counselors and psychologists, with their strong background in child development and problem solving, are in an excellent position to be effective school reform agents. Support service professionals can be most effectively employed within schools and in integrated teams that focus on solving system problems in addition to meeting individual level needs. In this capacity, support services can positively alter the school climate to support and achieve positive change in students' attitudes, behaviors, learning and achievement.

REFERENCES

Abec, J. M. (1987). Mental health consultation in schools: A developmental perspective. *School Psychology International,* 8(2–3), 73–77.

Adelman, H. (1993). School linked mental health interventions: Toward mechanisms for service coordination and integration. *Journal of Community Psychology, 21*(4), 309–319.

Adelman, H. (1996). Restructuring education support services intergrating community resources: beyond the full service school model. *School Psychology Review,* 25(4), 431–445.

Bailey, W. R., Deery, N. K., Gehrke, M., Perry, N. (1989). Issues in elementary school counseling: Discussion with American School Counselor Association Leaders. *Elementary School Guidance &Counseling,* 24(l), 4–13.

Boger, J. M (1990). The mental health team: A process of maximizing human potential in schools. *Paper presented at the annual meeting if the American Educational Research Association.*

Carnagie Task Force on Learning in the Primary Grades. (1996). *Years of Promise: A Comprehensive Learning Strategy for America's Children.* New York: Carnegie Corporation.

Carroll, B. (1993). Perceived roles and preparation experiences of elementary counselors: suggestions for change. *Elementary School Guidance & Counseling, 27,* 216–226.

Clancy, J. (1995). Ecological school social work: The reality and the vision. *Social Work in Education, 17*(l), 40–47.

Comer, J. P., Haynes, N. M., Joyner, E. T., Ben-Avie, M. (eds.). (1996). *Rallying the Whole Village: The Comer processfor reforming education.* New York: Teachers College Press.

Comer, J. P., Haynes, N. M. (1996b). Improving Psychoeducational Outcomes for African American Children. *Child and Adolescent Psychiatry: A comprehensive textbook,* Melvin Lewis (ed.). Baltimore: Williams & Wilkins, 1097–1103.

Comer, J. P., Haynes, N. M. (1995). School consultation: A psychosocial perspective. *Psychiatry, 2*(70), 1–13.

Conoley, J., Conoley, C. W. (1991). Collaboration for child adjustments: Issues for the school and clinic based child psychologists. *Journal of Consulting & Clinical Psychology, 59*(6), 821–829.

Curtis, M. J. & Stollar, S. A. (1996). Applying principles and practices of organizational change to school reform. *School Psychology Review*, 25(4), 409–417.

Dolan, L. (1992). Models for integrating human services into the school. *Johns Hopkins University,* Center for Research on Effective Schooling for Disadvantaged Students, 30.

Dowling, E., Taylor, D. (1989).The clinic goes to school: Lessons leamt. *Maladjustment &Therapeutic Education*, 7(l), 24–29.

Dryfoos, J. G. (1993).Schools as places for health, mental health, and social services. *Teachers College Record, 94*(3), 540–567.

Dryfoos, J. G. (1994). Medical clinics in junior high school: Changing the model to meet demands. *Journal of Adolescent Health, 15*(7), 549–557.

Dwyer, K. P., Gorin, S. (1996). A national perspective of school psychology in the context of school reform. *School Psychology Review, 25*(4), 507–511.

Ehly, S. (1993). Overview of group intervention for special services providers. *Special Services in School, 8*(l), 9–38.

Elias, M. J. (1995). Primary prevention as health and social competence promotion. *Journal of Primary Prevention, 16*(8), 5–24.

Osher, D., & Hanley, T. (1996). Implications of the national agenda to improve results for children and youth with or at risk of serious emotional disturbance. *Special Services in School*, 7–35.

Osterweil, Z.O. (1988).

Peeks, B. (1993). Revolutions in counseling and education: a systems perspective in the schools. E*lementary School Guidance & Counseling, 27*, 245–251.

Purkey, W., & Aspy, D.N. (1988). The mental health of students: Nobody minds? Nobody cares? *Person-Centered Review, 3*(l), 41–49.

Reynolds, D. (1987).

Riley, R. (1996). Improving America's schools. *School Psychology Review, 25*(4), 477–484.

Roeser, R.W., Midgley, C., & Urdan, T. C. (1996). Perceptions of the school psychological environment and early adolescents' psychological and behavioral functioning in school: The mediating role of goals and belonging. *Journal of Educational Psychology, 88*(3), 408–422.

Romualdi, V. & Sandoval, J. (1995). Comprehensive school-linked services: Implications for school psychologists. *Psychology in the Schools, 32*, 306–317.

Schultz, E. W., Glass, R. M., & Kamholtz, D. (1987). School climate: psychological health and well-being in school. *Journal of School Health, 57*(10), 432–437.

Shaw, S. R., Kelly, D. P., Joost, J. C., & Parker-Fisher, S. J. (1995). School-linked and school based health services: A renewed call for collaboration between school psychologists and medical professionals. *Psychology in Schools, 32*(3), 190–201.

Sigston, A., Noble, J., Fuller, A., & O'Donaghue, S. (1989). Doing time or negotiating the effective use of educational psychologists. *Educational & Child Psychology*, 6(4, pt 2), 39–44.

Stratford, R. (1990). Creating a positive school ethos. *Educational Psychology in Practice*, 5(4), 183–191.

Talley, R. C. & Short, R. J. (1996). Schools as health delivery sites: Current status and future directions. *Special Services in School*, 37–55.

Talley, R. C.& Short, R. J. (1996). Social reforms and the future of school practice: Implications or American psychology. *Professional Psychology: Research and Practice*, 27(l), 5–14.

Thacker, J. (1994). Organizational cultures: How to identify and understand them. *Educational & Child Psychology*, 1(3), 11–2 1.

Tharinger, D. (1995). Roles for psychologists in emerging models of school related health and mental health services. *School Psychology Quarterly*, 10(3), 203–216.

Thomas, A. (1987). School psychologist: An integral member of the school health team. *Journal of School Health*, 57(10), 465–469.

Thomas, A., Orf, M., Levinson, E., & Pinciotti, D. (1992). Administrators' perseptions of school psychologists' roles and satisfaction with school psychologists. *Psychological Reports*, 71, 571–575.

Vesey, J. (1996). Team collaboration leads to a sense of community. *NASSP Bulletin*, 80(584), 31–35.

Wagner, W.G. (1994). Counseling with children: An opportunity for tomorrow. *Counseling Psychologist*, 22(3), 381–401.

Weinberg, R. B. (1989). Consultation and training with school-based crisis teams. *Professional Psychology: Research and Practice*, 20(5), 305–308.

Werthamer-Larsson, L. (1994). Methodological issues in school based services research. Special Section: Mental health services research with children, adolescents, and their families. *Journal of Clinical Child Psychology*, 23(2), 121–132.

Ysseldyke, J. & Geenen, K. (1996). Integrating the special education and compensatory education systems into the school reform process: A national perspective. *School Psychology Review*, 25(4), 418–430.

Zahner, G. E., Pawelkiewicz, W., DeFrancesco, J., & Adnopoz, J. (1992). Children's mental health service needs and utilization patterns in an urban conununity: An epidemiological assessment. *Journal of the American Academy of Child & Adolescent Psychiatry*, 31(5), 951–960.

Zaki, M., & Partok-Engel, R. (1984). School as agent for mental health socialization of the individual. *School Psychology International*, 5(3), 147–150.

Zins, J. E., Conyne, R. K., & Charlene, R. (1988). Primary prevention: Expanding the impact of psychological services in schools. *School Psychology Review*, 17(4), 542–549.

Chapter Four

Pathway Three:
Personalized Learning Communities

"Personalization is the respectful, empathic and challenging engagement of students, premised on the belief and expectation that each individual student, when treated with understanding and sensitivity, can and will experience, personal growth, enhanced beliefs of self-efficacy, school success and self-fulfIllment in a truly authentic learning community". (Haynes, 1994)

Many young people across America are failing to receive an education that is meaningful and useful for their development. This problem is, in part, due to the critical shortage of adults in schools who can successfully connect into the lives, goals, and perspectives of their students. It is estimated that children spend approximately 15,000 hours in school between the first and twelfth grades. These hours are spent in academic and social learning activities, and in interactions with adults and other children (Rutter, 1985). These early developmental experiences can help to positively shape children's self-concepts, their sense of efficacy, their understanding of the world which surrounds them, and their beliefs about their place and roles in their families, school, society, and in the larger world. Therefore, it is important to create learning environments that are supportive of the child's total development and that are responsive to their needs. Personalization can be used to help ground school stakeholders in the use of everyday relationships to allow schools to function well and produce successful students. The establishment of mechanisms in schools which foster sensitivity and caring, and provide preventive strategies for addressing academic and psychosocial concerns, helps to build resilience among children and youth and buffer them against many of the social ills which they confront daily. In short, a truly personalized learning environment helps children develop well and achieve at their highest levels of their potential.

Unfortunately, the goal of creating personalized school communities is often illusive. Many of the adults in today's schools do not truly know and understand the needs of their children. What is often missing from these schools is an emphasis on the role of relationships in establishing and maintaining school success. Meeting the goal of higher student achievement cannot consistently occur without first establishing the kinds of relationships and in-school structures that will support and promote positive development. Greater school efforts at personalization can help to bring out the best in a larger proportion of students, across a variety of developmental pathways. Teachers can use personalization techniques as a gateway into their academic curriculum. The positive climate that results from personalization can be built upon in the classroom for positive learning outcomes.

Several assumptions grow out of the above working conceptual definition of personalization. These assumptions form the basis of an explanation and rationale for including personalization as an essential element of the work in the effort by schools to help all students achieve school success. The assumptions are as follows:

1. each student is a unique human being with different developmental needs, and deserves to have his/her uniqueness and needs considered in an authentic learning expenence.
2. for meaningful and successful learning to occur, the school context and learning processes must be relevant to the lives of students.
3. a truly personalized learning experience helps students to fully develop their potential.
4. both contextual and operational dimensions of a truly personalized and authentic learning experience are inclusive of the culture, history and experiences of the cultural and ethnic membership and reference group to which each child belongs.
5. a truly personalized educational experience is possible but only when and where there are significant changes in policies, practices, and attitudes affecting teaching and learning in schools.
6. there are significant personal, and social benefits to be realized from providing students with truly authentic learning experiences with personalized curriculum, instruction and assessment (CIA) at the core.

EACH STUDENT IS UNIQUE

Students differ and possess their own sets of peculiarities and important attributes. These differences include, among others, learning styles, developmental level and needs, multiple intelligences, and cultural background and experiences.

LEARNING STYLES

Kornhaber (1994) discussed the importance of learning style differences as a consideration—in personalization. Her argument was that students approach learning in different ways, process information differently and have preferences for some modalities over others. Keefe and Languisd (1983) defined a learning style as:

> the composite of characteristic cognitive affective and physiological factors that serve as relatively stable indicators of how a learner perceives interacts with, and responds to the learning environment. It is demonstrated in that pattern of behavior and performance by which an individual approaches educational experiences. Its basis lies in the structure of neural organization and personality which both molds and is molded by human development and learning experiences of home, school and society. (p. 1)

Some researchers have attempted to match specific learning styles with learning enviromnents (Dunn and Dunn, 1978). Norris et al (1975) suggested that impulsive learners perform better in structured learning environments and reflective learners perform better in unstructured learning environments and in activities requiring inductive reasoning. Davey (1976) found that field-independent learners compared to field-dependent learners prefer discovery learning methods. Other learning style. dimensions which interact with contextual factors include abstract vs concrete, simultaneous vs sequential cognitive processing and cooperative vs competitive goal orientations. Because of the multiplicity of learning styles proposed, consideration of learning styles as a factor in personalization would necessitate the selection of a dimension or dimensions which yield the most helpful information.

DEVELOPMENTAL LEVEL AND NEEDS

Due to biological factors and social circumstances, children develop at varying rates and—in disparate ways along the six pathways proposed by Dr. Comer. No two children in anyone classroom are at exactly the same place developmentally. Well (1992) acknowledges that "there is no such thing as a homogeneous classroom. In effect every child is special, unique, and unlike all others". (p. 2). Because of this, it is important to personalize the learning experience of each child to address the child's educational needs in an appropriate and helpful way. The social networks into which children are born, and in which they are nurtured and socialized influence how well children develop and their readiness for and attitudes toward school Knowing and understanding the developmental profile of each child, as this relates to the child's learning in school, is important to be able to teach each child in a profound and authentic way. (Comer 1988) Gardner (1994) suggests that personalization may occur on a continuum with varying degrees of personal engagement being appropriate for different students and producing varying kinds of effects for different children. Thus, it may be possible to construct an inverted bell shape curve for each child with degree of personalized engagement on the horizontal axis and productivity on the vertical axis showing that diminishing productivity may result from over personalization, and little productivity may result from under personalization, that is from missing the point at which the optimum level of personalized engagement is best for a given child. The optimum equilibrium point in the interaction between degree of personalization and level of productivity would be different for each child. However, in order to know what that optimum degree of personalization is for each child, we must know each child well, and we know each child well only when we are willing and able to establish personal dialogue and contact.

MULTIPLE INTELLIGENCES

In his mind—expanding works *Frames of Mind* (1983) and *Multiple Intelligences: The Theory In Practice (1993)*. Howard Gardner offered the proposition that schools must learn to recognize and support the special abilities of students. Gardner and his colleagues at Project zero explore ways in which the curriculum, instruction and assessment (CIA) activities in schools can facilitate the full development of these abilities, Hatch (1993) noted:

> At least in part, the popularity of MI (Multiple Intelligences) can be attributed to the fact that people—either as teachers, parents or students—have seen first hand how the conventional educational system has failed to address the diverse needs and strengths of students. The MI perspective explodes the traditional impersonal notions that math and verbal abilities are the only basis for assessing and engaging children in learning in schools. It also challenges the sole use of traditional standardized tests as the basis for judging children's abilities. In challenging these traditionally exclusionary educa-

tional viewpoints and practices, MI provides valuable information for leveraging change. (p. 198)

CULTURAL DIVERSITY

As the American demographic landscape becomes more culturally diverse, schools are facing challenges to provide culturallysensitive and validating educational experiences to students from many cultural backgrounds. Gordon (1992) noted:

> At least two ongoing phenomena characterize the social fabric of the United States and have increasingly serious implications for our educational system. They are changing demographic characteristics of the U.S. population and the continuing democratization of the nation's public institutions. Recognizing these changes, educators are increasingly voicing the concern that the educational system reflect the diversity of human characteristics in the country. (p. 235)

Gordon (1992) further noted that the nation's "roots have changed over the past 200 years from 90% European and 10% persons from other regional groups (cumulatively) to approximately 50% European and 50% persons from other regions in the present period" (p. 235).

In 1990, approximately 31% of the school age population (under 18) in the United States were minority, (African-American, Hispanic, Native American, Asian) This was twice what it was in 1980 when minority youth comprised 15 % of the school age population. By 2020 the minority population under 18 is expected to grow to 50% of all youth in that age group (Miller, 1993) Given this shift in the racial, ethnic and cultural distribution of students in American public schools, educators are increasing their efforts to encourage cultural sensitivity among students and staff. As schools become increasingly pluralistic and multicultural, personalization through cultural programming, infused throughout the CIA, becomes increasingly important.

Boateng (1990) in explaining the importance of multicultural education asserted:

> Considering the importance of addressing the inequalities in the curriculum and of preparing all children effectively for a multicultural society, restructing classroom instruction to reflect the diversity of society seems to be a viable alternative. From the perspective of educational policy and practice, public education must seek whatever information the social sciences can provide—concerning the different socio-cultural system from which its children come. (p. 77)

The goals of multicultural education as explained by Boateng (1990) are clearly in line with the ideals of personalization that responsive school communities aspire to attain. The goals are to:

1. reach their potential by drawing on their cultural experiences and by helping them to view events from diverse cultural perspectives.
2. overcome their fear of diversity that leads to cultural misunderstanding and cultural encapsulation,
3. view cultural differences in an equalitarian mode rather than in an inferior-superior mode.
4. expand their conception of what it means to be human in a culturally diverse world and to develop cross cultural competency—the ability to function within a range of cultures.

The importance of sensitizing and preparing teachers to address the educational and developmental needs of cultural diverse students was also well articulated by the Holmes Group (1990).

They asserted:

> When teachers learn more about their students they can build learning communities that embrace rather than smother cultural diversity. Students do differ. Without stereotyping or prepackaged responses, such differences can become opportunities for richer learning. A main aim of teacher preparation, then, should be to prepare novice teachers for a career in which they will be able to draw upon students' diversity to make learning dynamic and interesting—for children and for themselves. We speak of celebrating diversity because we believe that the hallmark of a true learning community is its inclusiveness—where teachers take the responsibility for helping each child take part to his or her fullest. The idea of a learning community has special significance in a democracy where all must fmd their voice. (p. 35)

Each student's self-definition includes an element of his/her racial and cultural identity, and his/her self-worth includes an element of how that identity is valued and validated in the school context.

HOW PERSONALIZATION DEVELOPS

Personalization develops through the existence of structured opportunities for interaction. These ongoing interactions among school stakeholders contribute to student development across multiple pathways and opportunities for growth. The systemic approach to personalization has seven basic premises.

1. A child's overall development is influenced by his or her interactions with significant adults.
2. The transition from family to school is influenced by the ability and willingness of educators and parents to manage the challenges that emerge when there is divergence between the culture of the school and the culture of the home.
3. The ability of parents and educators to facilitate academic learning rests on a relationship between adults and children, that is characterized by trust, support, positive regard, high expectations, affiliation and bonding.
4. Adults and children are able to best meet their responsibilities in a supportive climate that emphasizes a no fault approach to identifying and solving problems, decision making processes that generate consensus, and structures that promote collaborative working relationships.
5. The best decisions about programs and strategies, including curricula are made based on the careful analysis of qualitative data about the characteristics and needs of students.
6. The welfare of the child becomes the concern of all significant adults in the child's life and programs and activities are planned, implemented, and evaluated on the basis of their benefit to children.
7. Adult decision makers choose programs that fit students rather than conclude that there is something inherently wrong with students when children do not benefit from programs.

These premises suggest that effective and personalized education requires that educators and other adults who influence children's development should understand child development issues and be able to have this understanding reflected in the school's curriculum, pedagogy, and social activities.

The personalization approach uses a holistic strategy that addresses all aspects of school life including the academic social climate and school organization. It is a process that focuses on the total achievement of students in a climate of sensitivity, caring and challenge. It seeks to develop creative ways of dealing with problems, and to implement these ways using the collective good judgment (based on social and behavioral science knowledge) of school staff, parents, and the community.

Student, Social, Emotional and Academic Team

In personalized learning communities, there is a mechanism and a process for systematically addressing students' needs. This mechanism is often in the form of a Social, Emotional and Academic Team (SEAT) and is known by different names. The members of SEAT often include: (1) school psychologist,

(2) guidance counselor, (3) school nurse, (4) special education teacher, (5) attendance officer, (6) pupil personnel workers, and any other appropriate staff persons. The function of the SEAT is to address school wide climate and psychosocial issues that are likely to have an impact on the students' adjustment and life path choices. The SEAT also deals with individual student concern issues that are referred to it by teachers and staff. The SEAT is intended to act in a preventive, preemptive way rather than in a reactive, treatment fashion. It works in this fashion in providing on-going consultation to teachers and other staff in matters that pertain to child development and behavior. The SEAT helps the school to:

- apply child development and relationship knowledge and skills to the social climate, academic, and staff development programs developed by the governance and management body;
- facilitate the many interactions between parents and school staff;
- consult with classroom teachers to assist them in responding to students in a manner promoting growth and development;
- assist classroom teachers in developing strategies that prevent minor problems from becoming major ones;
- set up individualized programs for children with special needs which may involve the utilization of services outside of the school when necessary and possible;
- assist all staff members in bridging the gap between special education and regular classroom activities;
- provide consultation and training workshops to staff and parents on child development, human relations, and other mental health issues, and;
- make recommendations for building level policy changes designed to prevent problems.

Parent Involvement

It is widely acknowledged that meaningful parent involvement is an important element in a school's efforts to personalize teaching children's educational experiences and for student success. Parent involvement is intended to encourage parent participation at all levels of school life. The majority of parents serve at the first level, which involves general support activities, including attendance at PTA, PTO or PTSA meetings, social events and other school activities. At the second level, some parents serve in the building, as volunteer aides or assistants, in the library, cafeteria or in classrooms. Level three involves parents who are selected by the larger parent group to represent them on the school's governing council. As members of the Council, parents serve as vehicles for transmitting the views and opinions of the general parent body on issues related to academic, social and staff development needs of the school. In these ways, the Parent Program helps to bridge the gap between home and school. It reduces the dissonance that disadvantaged students can experience as they attempt to make adjustments from one environment to the other. By empowering parents, schools provide continuity in the socio-educational lives of children. This can also serve to strengthen families and help them build resilience in support of their children's academic and social development. Parental involvement is the cornerstone for success in developing a school environment that stimulates the total development of its students. Parents are expected to:

- select their representative to serve on the governance and management team;
- review the school plan developed by the governance and management group (School Council);
- work with staff in developing and carrying out activities of the parent-teacher general membership group (PTA, PTO) in line with the overall school plan; and
- support the efforts of the school to assist students in their overall development.

It is important to create a good school climate. In a personalized school, the school becomes a well functioning social system where the developmental needs of students can be addressed. All children need to develop a sense of adequacy and efficacy to be successful. Their search for an identity intensifies as they mature and their aggressive energies need to be channeled into constructive and wholesome activities. They benefit from cooperative and collaborative activities such as participating in community based projects. Such involvement increases resistance to negative and destructive influences in their proximal social environment. With its emphasis on social development and positive relationships, the personalization process is seen as an effective socio-educational intervention for empowering schools to positively influence the life paths of students.

It is through this kind of "whole village" approach that a school's staff personalize the schooling process towards meeting the individual and collective psycho-educational needs of all children. It is our proposition that schools alone cannot and should not be expected to address all of a child's developmental needs. The meaningful involvement of parents, and support from the wider community are essential to school's ability to educate children well. When parents and the wider community become full partners in children's education and development, a more holistic educational approach is possible, because many of the significant adult stakeholders in children's development become engaged in providing essential services to children and families. In the systemic approach schools are organized to allow for the full involvement and participation of all staff, parents and students in the life of the school. Members of the wider community are also involved in the process of developing and nurturing children through the schooling process. The positive climate established at school-wide levels can be built upon by teachers in the classroom for positive learning outcomes.

At the heart of the systemic process for helping schools to become more personalized are the respectful and mutually supportive relationships among adults in schools, including staff, parents and other adults from the community. Children learn from observing how the significant adults in their lives interact with one another and with children; how decisions are made and executed; and how problems are solved. They also learn from how adults treat them as children, and how much effort is given to ensure that their psychosocial and academic needs are totally met. The emphasis on the school being an interactive community helps to legitimize the teacher (and other adults) as sources of knowledge in the classroom. Additionally, the inclusion of students as sources of knowledge in their own right helps to personalize the flow of information between teacher and student. This kind of flexibility in both the school and classroom environments can yield positive learning gains for students.

The most effective relationships are those which are based on feelings of mutual empowerment and a keen sense of individual and collective efficacy. School staff, parents, and members of the wider community are seen as equal partners in the process of school improvement. The relationships among students themselves are very important sources of motivation and affirmation. Children who feel socially connected to school, and who derive positive self-affirmation from interactions with peers, are more likely to be motivated and to want to attend school. If the peer culture is one that values pro-social behavior, academic learning, and achievement, the connected student would be more likely to want to be an achiever. The school culture, however, must send positive messages about what it means to be a student, teacher or parent at that school in order to both promote and realize significantly positive psychosocial and academic growth (Pallas, 1988).

An essential element in student development through personalization is recognition and reinforcement of the home-school partnership. When children observe that home and school are engaged in a respectful partnership for their benefit, children are likely to develop more positive attitudes toward school and to do much better school work compared to situations in which school and home are seen as being "worlds apart". Although several impediments to meaningful parent involvement in the educational process are often cited, our experience is that significant and meaningful parent involvement is possible, desirable and valuable in improving student growth and performance. Essential to educational empowerment and school-based decision-making is the recognition that parents have much to offer if provided the opportunities to do so.

In many schools, parents are involved in many ways. They are encouraged to provide broad-based support for their children's education. This support can be in the form of encouraging children to complete homework assignments, attending parent-teacher conferences, and being actively involved in their school's parent-teacher association or organization. Parents are also directly involved in the daily life of the school by volunteering and serving as teacher aides, lunchroom monitors, library assistants, and office assistants. This level of involvement advances the personalization process by bringing parents in direct contact with staff and students in respectful, constructive and supportive ways. Children observe and learn from parents and staff working together as collaborators and partners for their benefit. Studies indicate that students benefit academically and psychosocially from this kind of parent participation. The connection between home and school is strengthened when parents are involved in helping to make decisions about school policies and procedures, together with school administrators and staff, through their representatives on the school council. This process allows parents to bring knowledge about their children's developmental and educational needs to the planning and designing of school and classroom activities.

The wider community, including businesses, social agencies, the media, local universities and colleges, health centers and hospitals, and community service organizations, should be part of a service network to schools and families to strengthen their capacity to meet the total developmental needs of children. Even with strong school councils, and helpful psychosocial support teams, many schools recognize the need for and importance of establishing linkages with community agencies and groups to enhance their effectiveness. Education, increasingly, is being regarded as a community enterprise with vital services coalesced into a support network that is available to children and families either directly or through the schools. This is a pivotal service due to parents' natural tendency to turn to schools for help or guidance on matters affecting their children. In addition, the multifaceted nature of education warrants that schools should have access to services which enhance the educational process and the ability of students to learn well. For example, businesses can offer internships, mentorship, or material resources, or to volunteer time in the school at least once per month or on some other interval schedule.

Social and community agencies may also assist by providing counseling and other social support to families or by contributing expertise to a school's psychosocial support team. Local universities and colleges contribute in many ways including providing pre- and in-service adult development training to teachers, counselors, psychologists, administrators and social workers, to prepare and assist them in addressing the psychosocial needs of children and families.

Personalization is a means of adapting the school environment to the needs, perspectives, and concerns of the individuals being taught. In personalizing teaching and learning, the school builds and strengthens the capacity within schools to address the total development of all children. This is accomplished through a process of empowerment that establishes true collaboration and mutual respect among all the significant adults in children's lives, including school staff, parents, other members of children's families, and significant others in their communities. Children themselves are respected and taught to respect others, their peers and the adults in their lives.

Essential services to children and their families are structured, coordinated and made more accessible, with schools playing a pivotal role. Schools alone cannot completely educate children, neither can families alone. But working together we can prepare our children well to face the future effectively and successfully.

The participation of school, parent and community stakeholders in an ongoing collaboration is an important component for school success with developing children, particularly in districts with diverse student populations. Increased appreciation by all school stakeholders of the perspectives, values, and viewpoints across their school community can lead to more effective, authentic, and relevant classroom pedagogy. Parents can become engaged in the educational enterprise in meaningful ways which empower them to be a more powerful and positive force in shaping their children's development. Homes, schools and communities become connected together in a support network that is designed to personalize the educational process and help children to develop holistically.

REFERENCES

Comer, J. P. (1980) School Power. New York: Free Press.

Comer et al (1999). Child by child: The Comer process for change in education. New York; teachers college press.

Gardner, H. (1993). Multiple intelligence: The theory in practice. New York: Basic Books.

Gardner, H. (1991). The unschooled mind: How children learn and how schools teach. New York: Basic Books.

Gardner, H., (1983). Frames of mind: The theory of multiple intelligences. New York: Basic Books.

Gardner, H. (1994). Cemments During ATLAS Seminar Review meeting. Cambridge: Harvard University.

Gergen, R. (1991). The saturated self: Dilemmas of identity in contemporarv life. Basic Books.New York.

Gordon, E. (1992). Conceptions of africentrism and multiculturalism in Education: A general overview. *Journal of Negro Education*, Ql, (3), 235–236.

Hatch, T. (1993). From research to reform. *Educational Horizons*, 11, (4), 197–202. Finding better ways to put theory into practice.

Haynes, N., Comer, J. P. & Roberts, V. (1993). A developmental and systems' approach to mental health in schools. *Educational Horizons, 71*(4), p. 181–186.

Haynes, N. M. and Gebreyesus, S. (1992). Cooperative Learning: A case for African-American students. *School Psychology Review*, 21, (4).

Haynes, N. M. and Comer, J. P. (1990). Helping black children succeed: The significance of some social factors. In R. Lomotey (Ed.). *Going to school: The African-American Experience*. (pp. 103–112). State University of New York Press.

Hirsch, E. D. (1988). Cultural Literacy: What every American needs to know. New York: Vintage Books.

Holland, B. (in press). Providing positive male role models for young black inner-city males in the primary grades. *Journal of Equity and Excellence*.

Holmes Group (1990). Tomorrow's schools: Principles for the design of Professional Development schools. East Lansing: Michigan State University.

Joyner, E., Haynes, N., & Comer, J. (1994). School development program nine step guide. New Haven: Yale Child Study Center.

Keefe, L. W. and Languis, M. L. (1983). *Operational Definitions*. NASSP Learning Styles Task Force, Reston, Va.: NASSP.

Komhaber. M. (1994). *Personalization: A Preliminary Conceptual Framework*. Cambridge: Harvard University. Project Zero.

McCombs, B. L. (1988). *What. is the relationshig between motivation and self-regulated learning?* Paper presented at the annual meeting of the American Educational Research Association, New Orleans.

Miller, L. S. (1993). Some Strategic Minority Education Issues and Possible Research and Policy Organization Initiatives To Respond To These Issues. Unpublished.

Norris, R. A, Hiekkmin, M. and Armstrong, T., (1975). Alternatives for individualized biology: The importance of cognitive style and conceptual complexity. *American Biology Teacher*, **n**, 293–297.

Pallas, A. M. (1988). School climate in American high schools. *Teachers College Press, 89*(4), 541–556.

Rutter, M. (1985). Family and school influences on cognitive development. *Journal of Psychology and Psychiatry, 26*(5), 683–704.

Schorr, L. with Schon, D. (1988). *Within our reach: Breaking the cycle of disadvantage*. New York: Anchor Press, Doubleday.

Sizer, T. (1992). Horace's school: redesigning the American High School. New York: Houghton Mifflin Company.

Spillane, M. (1993). SDP at 25: The pioneers speak: Remembering the early days. School Development Program Newsline. 2, (2), 1–3.

U.S. Department of Education (1987). Washington, D.C. What Works: Research About Teaching: and Learning.

Well, D. (1992). The key to each child's heart. The Jewish Special Educator, 1, (1) 2.

Zeuli, J. T. (1986). The Use of the Zone of Proximal Development in Education and School Contexts: A Vygotsls;yian Critigye. Paper published by the Institute for Research on Teaching. Michigan State University.

Chapter Five

Pathway Four: Increasing Students' Interest, Achievement, and Motivation (with Jodi Shydlo)

Many teachers face the daily challenge of motivating their students to learn, have interest in school work, and achieve to the best of their potential. One of the major motivational blocks is negative self-concept, or the child's negative self-image about their capabilities, efficacy, and worth as a person (McCombs & Whisler, 1997). Student's beliefs about themselves and their general abilities significantly influence their interest, achievement, and motivation (Madden, 1997). The problem educators face is this; how does one go about increasing positive self-concept in children so as to increase interest, motivation, and achievement in school?

The Interest, Achievement and Motivation group process was designed by the present author to enhance children's sense of connectedness to school and a purpose for being there. It addresses the problem of low academic performance and school disaffection among children by endeavoring to increase positive self-concept and students' belief and confidence in their potential to be successful in school. This increase in self-confidence (or, self-concept regarding students' capabilities and efficacy) is likely to also increase success-oriented behaviors and improve academic performance.

WHAT IS THE I AM GROUP PROCESS?

The "I AM" group process is an eight week program of developmental guidance lessons for a whole class of students. It can also be conducted as a series of small group sessions with a similar curriculum of developmental guidance lessons. Each group session is designed to emphasize a particular theme in terms of social skills, school interest, achievement, and motivation.

Affirmations are recited at the beginning each session to help students internalize positive messages about themselves such as "I am a good person" and "I will succeed." The goals of the group are:

1. To encourage among students a positive sense of self and belief in their potential to achieve at high levels in school.
2. To support and reinforce achievement-related behaviors among students.
3. To encourage and support positive attitudes towards school and work among students.
4. To increase students' achievement motivation and influence their academic performance.
5. To reinforce prosocial values, attitudes and behavior.

WHY IS THIS GROUP PROCESS IMPORTANT?

This group process is important because when students accept and internalize the "I AM" message that they are valuable, capable people, they show greater interest in school work and are more highly motivated to achieve. It is important for educators to find ways to stimulate students' interest, enhance their motivation, and provide them with the behavioral and cognitive tools that they need to realize their fullest achievement potential. Motivation has been defined as "the desire to achieve a goal that has value for the individual" (Linskie, 1997). Achievement motivation is a person's internal desire to succeed and is generally accompanied by a need to avoid failure and an effort on the person's part to be successful A positive relationship between achievement motivation and academic performance has been indicated in past studies (Jegede, 1997). This is the reason why it is an important concept that is stressed in the "I AM" group process.

In addition to achievement motivation, the positive relationship between self-esteem and academic performance has also been supported by the literature (Meece, Blumenfeld, & Hoyle, 1988; Nichols, 1996; Nichols and Miller, 1994; Nichols and Utesch, 1998). Self-esteem is defined by Woolfolk (1995) as how we evaluate our self-concept and the value we place on our behaviors and capabilities. Students with high self-esteem (or, positive self-concept) are more likely to be successful academically, have better attitudes toward and greater interest in school, more positive classroom behavior, and popularity amongst peers (Marsh, 1990; Mecalfe, 1981; Nichols and Utesch, 1998; Reynolds, 1980). For the reasons listed above, the promotion of positive self-concept is an integral part of the "I AM" group process and is one of the dependent variables being examined in this study.

One of the concepts addressed in the "I AM" group process is goal-setting or, rather, how to plan long and short-term goals. Madden (1997) investigated how 126 elementary teachers motivated their students to do effective goal setting. Important conclusions made from this study include:

1. "Students work more diligently on self-made goals than from the expectations of other."
2. "Children who feel self-efficacy (competence or power) in reaching goals show effort and persistence."
3. "Children who know that they can reach their highest goals are more motivated to work toward them."
4. Children are more motivated to work toward goals they can obtain quickly. (Madden, 1997).

Thus, the "I AM" group process stresses the idea of creating personal goals and through the promotion of positive self-concept, it is hoped that they will feel efficacious in achieving their goals.

According to Piers (1984), children's self reports have not always significantly corresponded with teacher ratings. However, later studies have confirmed the positive relationship between students' self-concept and academic achievement and teachers' expectations (Good & Brophy, 1987; Haynes, 1996). Therefore, a teacher school behavior rating form was prepared for this study to evaluate how teachers expect their students to perform in school. The relationship between self-concept (as measured by the Piers-Harris Children's Self-Concept Scale) and teacher expectations (as measured by the teacher rating form) will be examined in this study.

McCombs (1997) discussed how negative self-concept and feelings of insecurity about one's efficacy can thwart a child's enthusiasm and normal intrinsic motivation to learn. Whether students attribute their successes in school to external versus internal factors (e.g. poor studying versus poor intelligence) has an effect on motivation. If a child internally believes that he or she is not smart or capable, motivation to succeed and school achievement can drop.

One way to bolster positive self-concept that is used in this study is to recite affirmations. According to Canfield and Wells (1994), an affirmation "asserts a desired condition or objective as though it were already a reality" (p. 234). An affirmation has six essential components: "It's personal, it's positive, it's specific, it's visual, its present tense, and it's emotional." (Canfield & Wells,1994, p. 234). An example of an affirmation might be, "I do very well at solving word problems in math!"

It is recognized that peer, parent, and teacher support have important effects on student self-concept, motivation and achievement. One roadblock to support on any of these levels can be poor social skills and behaviors. In a re-view study of social skills interventions conducted by Zaragoza, Vaughn, and McIntosh (1991), students with behavior problems are more likely to be re-jected by their peers and targeted for teacher reprimand than by peers who be-have normally. Thus, the "I AM" process addresses the issue of proper social behavior. In each classroom, there are always some students who can use les-sons in proper social skills.

Hootstein's (1996) RISE (Relevance, Interest, Satisfaction, and Expecta-tions) model for motivating at-risk students to learn emphasizes concepts such as use of positive self-talk (affirmations), realistic and personal goal-set-ting in order to gain a sense of accomplishment, satisfaction, and efficacy, and teacher support to bolster motivation. All of these concepts are important components in the "I AM" group process.

The RISE model is relevant to this study in that the "I AM" group also looks at student interest and students expectations (or self-concept) about their ability to succeed. Additionally, this study also looks at at-risk students, or, students at-risk (by virtue of poverty, neighborhood safety, low self-esteem, boredom in school, poor health, etc.) of not achieving their full po-tential in school. Students who are bored due to the lack of a connection they see between their learning and outside lives may be perceived as unmotivated when they are simply yearning for more real-life relevant learning material (Hootstein, 1996) Another example of a motivation group model is Magliocca's and Robinson's (1991) "I Can" strategy for promoting self-confidence. Magliocca and Robinson (1991) emphasize immediately identi-fying and praising positive behavior, breaking problems down into smaller steps (addressed in the "I AM" problem-solving class session), and encour-aging risk-taking. For example, a student may be praised immediately for raising her hand before speaking. Or, students are told that it's okay to take a risk and make a mistake because we all make mistakes and can learn from them (Magliocca & Robinson, 1991). These ideas and concepts were utilized during the "I AM" group process.

GROUP PROCEDURE

The "I AM" group process is an eight-week program of developmental guid-ance lessons for a whole class of students. The class is run once a week for an hour each session. The weekly themes and curriculum are as follows:

At the start of each group session, the group members recite a set of positive affitmations such as, "I am a good person"; "I will do my best to succeed". Dur-ing week one the purpose of the group is explained and the expectations and group rules are discussed. During week two, the theme is goal setting and we teach students how to set and achieve long-term and short-term goals. They draw themselves as they might see themselves when they grow up. Also, the group members are given a ditto sheet with footsteps so they can define the steps they need to take to achieve their goals. During week three the theme is problem solving and each child gets a handout with general information about how to solve problems. Group members are taught to play the game of chess with the class as an example of a problem-solving activity. During week four the theme is social skills training and assertiveness. Group members view a video titled "How to Say 'No' Without Losing Your Friends" which provides some assertiveness training. After watching the video, the group discusses how to deal with peer pressure and help answer personal questions about how to be assertive in various situations. During week five, the group the theme is about school attendance, doing well on class work, homework, and test taking. Students are given handouts on this topic and they discuss the importance of good attendance and good study/work habits. During this week the principal comes in and gives a motivational speech to the class about their potential, the importance of a good education, and to offer encouraging praise. This allows the children to see the principal in a different role other than that of disciplinarian. During week six, the theme is about respecting others' feelings and how the children's self-esteem is affected by others. Vignettes about typical social situations are analyzed and appropriate ways to act in those situations are discussed. The class also talks about how students feel when they are laughed at, made fun of, or praised. During week seven, the theme is about getting in touch with one's own emotions and how to communicate them. Students are encouraged to express their feelings in appropriate ways and they talk about the importance of communicating hurt feelings as opposed to acting out with aggression. Classical music is played and students are asked to draw or write how they are feeling that day. The music is designed to help students relax and to concentrate on their inner feelings. During week eight, there is a graduation ceremony and students are presented with a reward certificate for completing the "I AM" group.

IMPACT OF THE I AM PROCESS

Focus groups after the group process has ended can provide information about how students and teachers feel about the class and how they feel the class affected them. While we did have a discussion at the end of each group process about these topics, it was informal and not a structured focus group. Children and teachers gave positive feedback which is not revealed in this study's data analysis.

Upon consultation with others about the group process, it was proposed that perhaps this process is most effective as a yearlong motivational piece that should be incorporated into the class curriculum. However, this study and past studies have shown that short-term group processes can have a significant effect if implemented properly (Page & Chandler, 1994). Page and Chandler (1994) had significant results after conducting two different self-concept enhancing groups that each ran for 2 hours per week for 10 weeks. It is a question of how long the group process is, how well it is implemented, and what outside factors could be affecting the student sample.

During class discussions, students have expressed positive feelings about reciting affirmations and usually recited them with enthusiasm. At face value, it seemed that this group was having some positive impact on the students. This could be seen in the joy many students expressed at the start of each "I AM" class and by the comments students made during and at the end of the group process. Students generally expressed that while the class did not improve 100% after the group process, there was an improvement in their overall feeling of positive self-concept. In a few cases, this was not true; there are always students for whom a positive class experience is not enough to boost positive self-concept. Generally, students were more aware of the positive impact of saying affirmations and realizing one's strengths. They said that they felt "better" and felt "good" when stating these affirmations.

REFERENCES

Alderman, M. K. (1990). Motivation for at-risk students. *Educational Leadership*, *48*(1), 27–31.

Ames, N. L. (1994). *Changing Middle Schools: How to Make Schools Work for Young Adolescents.* San Francisco, CA: Jossey-Bass Publishers, Inc.

Boggiano, A. K. & Pittman, T. S. (1992). Achievement and motivation: A social-developmental perspective (Eds.). New York, NY: Cambridge University Press.

School Failure. Norwood, MA: Christopher-Gordon Publishers, Inc.

Improving the Social Skills of Children and Youth with Emotional and Behavioral Disorders. Reston, VA: Council for Children with Behavioral Disorders.

Canfield, J., & Wells, H. C. (1994). *101 Ways to Enhance Self-Concept in the Classroom.* Needham Heights, MA: Allyn and Bacon behavior in children. *Early Childhood Research Quarterly, 4,* 51–60. children. *Educational Leadership, 53*(1), 37–40.

Comer, J. P. (1998) Educating poor minority children. *Scientific American, 259*(5), 42–48.

Good, T. L., & Brophy, J. E. (1987). *Looking in Classrooms.* (4th ed.) New York: Harper & Row.

Haynes, N. M. (1996). Creating safe and caring communities: Comer school development program schools. *Journal of Negro Education, 65*(3), 308–314.

Hilliard, A. G., & Lomotey, K. (Ed.) (1990). *Going to School.* Albany, NY: Suny Press.

Hootstein, E. W. (1996). The RISE model: Motivating at-risk students to learn. *Clearing House, 70*, 97–100.

Jegede, J. O. (1997). Effects of achievement motivation and study habits on Nigerian secondary school students' academic performance. *Journal of Psychology Interdisciplinary & Applied, 131*(5), 523–529.

Linskie, R. (1977). *The Learning Process: Theory and Practice.* New York: D. Van Nostrand Company.

Madden, L. E. (1997). Motivating students to learn better through own goal-setting. *Education, 117*(3), 411–415.

McCombs, B. L. (1997). *The Learner-Centered Classroom and School.* San Francisco, CA: Jossey–Bass Publishers, Inc.

Magliocca L. A. & Robinson, N. M. (1991). The "I Can" Strategy for Promoting Self-Confidence. *Teaching Exceptional Children, 23*(2), 30–33.

Marsh, H. W. (1990). Influences of internal and external frames of reference on the formation of math and English self-concepts. *Journal of Educational Psychology, 82*, 107–116.

Meece, J., Blumenfeld, P., & Hoyle, R. (1988). Student goal orientations and cognitive engagement in classroom activities. *Journal of Educational Psychology, 80*, 514–523.

Metcalfe, B. (1981). Self-concept and attitude toward school. *British Journal of Educational Psychology, 51*, 66–76.

Nichols, J. (1996). The effects of cooperative learning on student achievement and motivation in high school geometry class. *Contemporary Educational Psychology, 21*, 467–476.

Nichols, J., & Miller, R. (1994). Cooperative learning and student motivation. *Contemporary Educational Psychology, 19*(2), 167–178.

Nichols, J. D., & Utesch, W. E. (1998). An alternative learning program: Effects on student motivation and self-esteem. *The Journal of Educational Research, 91*(5), 272–278.

Page, R. C., & Chandler, J. (1994). Effects of group counseling on ninth-grade at-risk students. *Journal of Mental Health Counseling, 16*(3), 340–351.

Piers, E. V. (1969). *The Piers-Harris Children's Self-Concept Scale.* Nashville: Counselor Recordings and Tests.

Piers, E. V. (1984). *Piers-Harris Children's Self-Concept Scale: Revised Manual* Los Angeles, CA: Western Psychological Service in motivation and cognition in students with and without learning disabilities.

Reynolds, W. M. (1980). Self-esteem and classroom behavior in elementary school children. *Psychology in the Schools, 17*, 273–277.

Rossi, R. J. (1994). *Schools and Students at Risk: Context and Framework for Positive Change.* New York: Teachers College, Colombia University Press.

Woolfolk, A. E. (1995). *Educational Psychology.* (6th ed.). Boston, MA: Allyn & Bacon.

Zaragoza, N., Vaughn, S., & McIntosh, R. (1991). Social skills interventions and children with behavior problems: A review. *Behavioral Disorders, 16*(4), 260–275.

Chapter Six

Pathway Five: School Climate Factors That Support School Success

Increased violence and conflicts of all types within the school environment has sent an alarming call to educators to more carefully and consistently address students' social and emotional needs. Administrators with the support of classroom teachers, school counselors, school psychologists, school social workers and other support staff, are now considering how best to address the developmental needs of the whole child in school. Traditionally children's social and emotional development has received scant attention from educators because it has been seen as mainly the purview of parents. Yet current research supports the assertion that children do much better academically when their social and emotional needs are addressed in a systematic way as part of the school's curriculum and organized activities (Comer, Haynes, Joyner, & Ben-Avie, 1996).

Students who experience overall school success, tend to demonstrate higher levels of what Goleman calls "emotional intelligence" than their less successful peers. There are two major dimensions to "emotional intelligence" these are internal and external dimensions (Goleman, 1995). The internal dimension is concerned with the student's capacity to recognize, monitor, manage and express his or her feelings in appropriate and healthy ways. The external dimension is concerned with the student's capacity to interact in socially acceptable ways with peers and adults. This includes being aware of the feelings and needs of others and responding in appropriate ways. These two dimensions are consistent with Howard Gardner's notions of intrapersonal and inter-personal intelligences. Negative behaviors and school outcomes including school violence, dropout, disinterest and underachievement are linked to the social and emotional development of students in schools

(Elias, Zins, Weissberg, Frey, Greenberg, Haynes, Kessler, Schwabstone, & Shriver, 1997).

School administrators are the leaders most likely to direct the movement that will prepare children to succeed holistically including socially, emotionally and academically. Literature supports this generalization that social competence and psychological well-being are significantly related to academic achievement (Comer & Haynes, 1996). However, best practice appears to be more of a challenge in implementation for many schools. Therefore, it becomes our educational charge to provide strategies to students to empower them to succeed. Students can learn to the full extent of their abilities if they are under less psychological duress or can adjust well to stressful situations. Schools may address students' psychological and emotional development and their capacity to be resilient in difficult circumstances by helping students to develop their social and emotional skills. One important way for schools to accomplish this is by inviting and involving the input and expertise of significant adults (e.g. parents, educators and friends) in children's lives. Schools are optimal service delivery sites because of the number of students and families serve.

Schools are also very influential on children and youth growth because of the amount of time children spend in school. At least half of a child's developmental period is spent in school (Comer & Haynes, 1996). Educators need to assume responsibility for the developmental environment that they have direct control over, namely the school setting. School is the first opportunity professionals have to reinforce positive growth and development begun in the community and family or to compensate for underdevelopment (Osher & Haynes, 1996). This is important because primary care takers are either failing to recognize and prevent treatable problems, or are unable to handle them when they arise. Schools, then, become the critical system for children's support.

Within the context of the school environment, educators' roles and responsibilities are highly significant and the learning opportunities they provide (intentional and unintentional) have long-term influence in many facets of an individual child's growth (Talley & Short, 1996). During this period, it is especially important that children and youth establish a high level of attachment that enables adults to influence their behavior.

Although schools can have a positive influence on children, they can also have a negative impact. A child's mental health condition can become aggravated both by interactions in school and by the schooling itself. School-related stress plays a role in triggering predisposed conditions and may also elevate the potential for conflict. Psychological stress is high in schools for staff, students, and parents because of the many people involved in the educational process and because of different goals, motivations, and backgrounds of those within the school. The struggle to understand those many differences can be significant. Hence, variance in educational performance is not necessarily the result of differences in students' inherent ability to learn. Rather, these differences may be the result of the inability of many schools to respond to increasing needs of students who are under more social pressure (Comer, Haynes, Joyner, & Ben-Avie, 1996).

It is now time to address the needs of the whole learner; the child growing toward independence. As highly skilled professionals, principals, teachers and other educators recognize that the needs of children are not best addressed in isolation. Though educators have been quick to embrace new curricula and instructional methods, there has not been a similar eager response to embrace social and emotional learning strategies. Educators realize that children are failing, but reform mechanisms have mainly focused on increasing excellence through competency testing and cognitive skills work. These strategies do not help students, especially those at high risk, unless they are accompanied by strong support services in a caring and developmentally sensitive school climate. School reform efforts will be more effective where underlying developmental and social issues are adequately addressed (Carnegie Task Force on Learning in the Primary Grades, 1996). This emphasis on increasing test scores has caused a neglect of affective education and developmental concerns that affect students. Reform efforts will be costly and ineffective as long as their underlying developmental and social issues remain unaddressed.

HOW SHOULD SCHOOLS ADDRESS THE SOCIAL PROBLEMS AND PSYCHOLOGICAL STRESS CHILDREN AND YOUTH FACE IN THEIR DAILY LIVES IN SCHOOL AND AT HOME?

Within schools are housed the leadership, professional expertise, and skills necessary to teach and model "best practices" both for academic learning and life skills. Educational leadership acknowledges the talents of its teams and is now called upon to utilize that talent in an increased capacity. Instead of servicing some children individually or in response to crisis as "special needs" arise, it is now time to address all children's needs holistically within the community of the school population. We know with certainty that each child has needs which must be addressed to ensure their success both within the school and outside of it in the larger society.

Mental health and support service providers, such as school counselors, psychologists and social workers, with administrators and teachers, make optimal school change agents within an ecological school reform approach. Their professional training gives them the background and skills to implement the child-centered reform processes previously discussed. In order for changes in any system to be effective, individuals who have expertise in planning, problem solving, and facilitating organizational change need to be involved in the planning and implementation of those changes (Carnegie Task Force on Learning in the Primary Grades, 1996). Counselors, psychologists and other support service providers are in the best position to fulfill this need for experts. They have the skills to sustain broad reform goals while still remaining within their field of expertise, as they target cognitive, affective, and structural components of the school system. If the reform goals are student centered, as they should be, schools need to rely on the competencies and input of counselors, psychologists and other professional support staff regardless of who is implementing the changes.

Ysseldyke & Geenen (1996) cite particular competencies that may be used by counselors and other support staff in supporting principals and other staff in meeting students' needs. Included are collaborative skills; communication, conflict management, and problem solving skills; individual and group counseling skills; consulting skills; diagnostic testing skills; and knowledge about child development and social issues.

Generally, educators are very much concerned with helping all children adjust well and succeed in school. There are many students who seem to naturally adapt to the school's program and who often do well or very well academically and socially. Those children on any measure of emotional intelligence tend to score at a very high level. Educators, for the most part, see these students as model students and a pleasure to teach. There are other children for whom the school experience is much more challenging and difficult and who often require much more attention and intervention. These students on any measure of emotional intelligence would probably score at a lower level, yet they have enormous academic and social potential that only needs to be recognized and developed. Where a school embraces a philosophy of responsibility for meeting the social and emotional needs of its student population, as well as their learning needs, children who have deficits in one or the other area may still find themselves included and their needs addressed.

Principals are often recognized by their colleagues, staff, students, and parents as instructional leaders. They are regarded as building leaders who set the tone and establish the climate and context for meaningful learning to occur. The principal's role in promoting social and emotional learning is not always as clear, in large part because the benefits of efforts to promote social and emotional learning in schools are also not always as clear as the benefits from academic and instructional efforts.

Yet, it has been demonstrated that school-based social and emotional learning programs enhance not only students' psychological and social well-being in schools but also their academic performance (Curtis & Stollar, 1996). Such programs improve students' ability to work well with others, enhance their social and academic problem solving skills; increase their achievement motivation; and generally raise their performance on standardized tests and other academic performance measures.

The relationship between students' social and emotional development and their academic development is a strong and inseparable one. Neuroscience has shown us that the emotional centers of the brain are closely and tightly connected to the academic centers of the brain. How students experience school and learning influences how students learn and achieve. Students do not compartmentalize themselves into academic school selves for the purpose of learning and social-emotional selves for the purpose of non-academic interactions. Learning and emotions are interconnected in neurological webs that neuroscientists are learning much more about. Academic stimuli when processed trigger emotional responses, pleasant or unpleasant. Emotional events when processed influence academic learning, positively or negatively (Haynes & Marans, 1999).

Many principals appreciate this implacable linkage between social and emotional development and learning and academic development and learning. They explore ways to enhance the total development of all students through a variety of curricular and programmatic activities in schools. They also foster and support a school climate that is nurturing of students' social, emotional and academic development and that challenges students to meet high academic and social standards.

One such principal is Ms. Lola Nathan, principal of the Davis Street Academy in New Haven Connecticut. She is an instructional leader and a student-development leader who is widely recognized for the effective manner in which she has blended academic development and social and emotional development activities throughout the school's culture and program. For example, Ms. Nathan has instituted a program called "essentials of literacy" which incorporates social skills development with literacy enhancement. Parents work as volunteers, side by side with the teacher and students at different computer reading stations. The process addresses basic reading skills in a climate of trust, support, nurturance, and challenge. Recent data indicate that students' reading performance has significantly improved as have their behavior and attitudes in the classroom (Haynes, 1999).

Another initiative that has shown significant promise at Davis Street Academy is the Interest, Achievement and Motivation (I AM) Group The purpose of the group is to increase students' interest in schoolwork, improve their academic achievement and enhance their motivation for success. The group is conducted with entire classrooms as developmental guidance classes or with smaller groups of students. Each session is 45 minutes. Each "I AM" intervention consists of eight sessions. At the end of the eight-week cycle with one class or group, another class or group begins the intervention. The first session is an introduction to the themes of interest, achievement and motivation of the students. The other sessions focus on specific social and academic skills such as decision-making, problem solving, studying and homework, work habits and attitudes in school, anger management and appropriate expressions of emotions and goal setting. At the end of the eight weeks, a graduation ceremony is held and students receive a certificate of completion which is presented by the principal and classroom teacher.

A POSITIVE SCHOOL CLIMATE IS ESSENTIAL

It is becoming more and more evident that in order to enhance students' social and emotional development and improve their academic performance, a positive and wholesome school climate is essential. Academic and social programs are most effective when introduced in a climate that is sensitive and responsive to students' developmental needs (Haynes & Comer, 1996).

As in the case of Davis Street Academy and West Mecklenburg High School, initiatives that most effectively promote social and emotional learning and high academic achievement are designed and implemented within school and classroom contexts and send a strong message that this is a school where students are respected, cared for, nurtured and challenged to do their best. The climate of the school should reflect a number of important dimensions. These dimensions include:

- *Order and Discipline*: A school with an orderly and disciplined school climate establishes clear guidelines and rules for students' conduct. The school provides opportunities for constructive and appropriate behaviors thus increasing acceptable pro-social behavior and reducing negative acting out behaviors.
- *Student Interpersonal Relations*: When students respect, trust and treat one another kindly, the likelihood of antisocial episodes in the school decreases. Additionally, students who are troubled by difficult experiences outside of the school may also feel safe and secure in their relationships with their fellow students.
- *Student-Teacher Relations*: Students often look to the adults in school for guidance, support and direction. The extent to which students experience a

sense of attachment and bonding with the adults has an impact on the level of order and discipline that exist in the school. In addition, children who are exposed to difficult life experiences outside of the school find themselves able to seek help from staff who care enough to listen and offer their support.

- *Fairness*: A major source of strife and conflict in many schools is the perceived or real problem of bias and unfair treatment of students on the basis of ethnicity, gender, social class, disability or some other factor. Students who attend schools where they are treated fairly and equally are less likely to experience fractional strife and feelings of isolation leading to violent episodes. Students, who feel that they are equally valued and have equal access to school resources, experience a sense of connectedness with school. They are more motivated to learn and less likely to act out their frustrations and vent their anger in aggressive ways.

- *Achievement Motivation*: There is a strong correlation between students' academic self-esteem, their motivation to learn and their behavior in school. Students who are focused on learning and achieving are less likely to get in trouble and exhibit behavior problems than children who are not connected and engaged in learning.

- *Parent Involvement*: Parents play an important role in helping to address issues and concerns of critical significance to students, families and schools. The presence of parental involvement provides the school with input from parents and reflects a culture that values parents as an important resource in efforts to prevent and address unhealthy social and emotional interactions.

- *Physical Conditions of the School Building*: The physical condition of the school building has an impact on students' liking of the school, their attachment to the school, their motivation to achieve and their behavior and achievement. The more pleasant, tidy, warm and challenging the school building, the less likely there are to be incidents of fighting and violence in the school.

- *Academic Focus*: As teachers and other staff challenge students to achieve academically, and involve them in creative and stimulating activities, the more likely students are to be immersed in productive learning activities and the less likely they are to be involved in destructive and harmful activities.

- *Caring and Sensitivity*: A caring and sensitive environment offers youth a safe and secure place where they may seek and receive help in dealing with painful experiences. Students adjust well and perform satisfactorily in schools where staff and fellow students are understanding, caring and helpful.

- *Collaboration*: When the adults in school, including parents, staff, and the administration, work collaboratively to improve schools for students, they provide models of cooperative work that students can observe and emulate. They also collectively develop programs that reduce conflict, enhance the spirit and culture of community and improve student adjustment and performance.
- *School-Community Relations*: Schools that have close ties to the larger community are positioned to access and benefit from the many valuable resources that the community has to offer. Community resources include: groups that provide mentors and role models for students, businesses that establish partnerships with schools and provide speakers and internship opportunities, health centers that provide professional staff to serve on the Student Staff Support Team that addresses behavioral and mental health issues. When there is a strong linkage between school and community, the conditions that lead to problem behaviors such as school violence are decreased and the opportunities to make a positive difference for children who are impacted by negative life experiences are heightened.
- *Staff Dedication To Student Learning*: The level of dedication of the school staff to help students develop well and realize their full potential has importance for students' adjustment and behavior in school. When student's sense genuine commitment to helping them achieve well in school they respond positively to adult authority figures and connect in meaningful ways with the learning activities in the school.
- *Staff Expectations*: Students' internalize the expectations that their teachers have of them and often behave in ways that are consistent with these expectations. When teachers believe that students can do well in school, they communicate these beliefs in various ways that enhance students' self-esteem and inspire them to want to achieve. Students who experience positive experiences and receive encouraging messages tend to behave and perform well. These students are likely to behave in socially desirable and constructive ways. These students are also likely to channel their energies in constructive activity and likely to earn the admiration and respect of their teachers.

In order to educate children and youth effectively, schools need to address the social and emotional factors, which affect children's learning capabilities. School principals, classroom teachers and support staff in partnership with parents are essential to the development of an effective response by their schools to meet students' social and emotional needs. It is through the leadership of the principals that climate is shaped and teams are formed. Professional support staff, with their strong background in child development and problem solving, are in an excellent position to be effective school reform agents. Utilized fully within schools, highly skilled support service professionals can be most effectively employed in integrated teams that focus on solving system problems in addition to meeting individual level needs. In this capacity, working with principals and instructional staff, professional support staff may directly address student social and emotional needs and enhance the school climate to support positive changes in students' attãitudes, behaviors and academic achievement

REFERENCES

Ben-Avie M. (1998). The school development program at work in three high schools. In N. Haynes (guest editor). *Journal of Education for Students Placed At Risk: Special Issue: Changing Schools for Changing Times: The Comer School Development program.* 53–70.

Carnegie Task Force on Learning in the Primary Grades. (1996). *Years of Promise: A Comprehensive Learning Strategy for America's Children.* New York: Carnegie Corporation.

Comer, J. P., Haynes, N. M. (1996b). *Improving psychoeducational outcomes for African American children. Child and Adolescent Psychiatry: A comprehensive textbook,* Melvin Lewis (ed.). Baltimore: Williams & Wilkins, 1097–1103.

Comer, J. P., Haynes, N. M., Joyner, E. T., Ben-Avie, M. (eds.). (1996). *Rallying the Whole Village: The Comer process for reforming education.* New York: Teachers College Press.

Comer, J. P., Haynes, N. M., Joyner, E. & Ben-Avie, M. (1996). *Rallying the whole village: The Comer process for reforming education.* New York: Teachers College Press.

Curtis, M. J. & Stollar, S. A. (1996). Applying principles and practices of organizational change to school reform. *School Psychology Review, 25*(4), 409–417.

Elias, M., Zins, J. Weissberg, R., Frey, K., Greenberg M., Haynes, N., Kessler, R., Schwabstone, M., & Shriver, T. (1997). *Promoting social and emotional learning: Guidelines for educators.10–25* Alexandria: Association for Supervision and Curriculum Development.

Goleman, D. (1995). *Emotional Intelligence: Why it can matter more than IQ.* New York: Bantam Books.

Haynes, N. M. & Comer, J. P. (1996). Integrating schools, families and communities through successful school reform. *School Psychology Review 25*(4), 10–25.

Haynes, N. M. (1999). *Changing times for changing schools: The Comer school development program.* Mahwah, New Jersey: Lawerence Erlbaum Associates.

Haynes, N. M. & Marans, S. (1999). Promoting tolerance and respect for differences in schools. In J. Cohen (ed.). *Social and emotional development: Passage through adolescence.* New York: Teachers College press.

Osher, D., & Hanley, T. (1996). Implications of the national agenda to improve results for children and youth with or at risk of serious emotional disturbance. *Special Services in School, 7*–35.

Talley, R. C. & Short, R. J. (1996). Schools as health delivery sites: Current status and future directions. *Special Services in School*, 37–55.

Ysseldyke, J. & Geenen, K. (1996). Integrating the special education and compensatory education systems into the school reform process: A national perspective. *School Psychology Review, 25*(4), 418–430.

Chapter Seven

Pathway Six: Fostering Resilience

If schools are to leave No Child Behind, then they must not only give children a good and healthy start in life but must also help them to meet life's challenges, overcome adversity and move forward in a positive and successful way. Resilience is concerned with individual variations in response to risk. Resilience among youth incorporates the feelings that youth possess about their ability to deal with life's challenges and their ability to influence and control what happens to them. Resilience is not a fixed attribute that resides within the individual nor is it an inherited trait. It is learned, developed, nurtured and supported by the environment, including the quality of social and developmental experiences that children have with significant adults in their lives. Resilience is the healthy, adaptive and effective response to trauma or stressful events leading to personal growth, a new level of awareness and increased capacity to face and succeed in meeting new challenges Resilience is, therefore, the successful, positive, self-enhancing and self-empowering resolution of the dynamic interplay between risk factors on one hand and protective factors on the other Youth who show high levels of social and emotional intelligence (SEI) and at least average cognitive and academic intelligence (CAI) in responding effectively and successfully to challenging and difficult situations including traumatic events, compared to youth who do not respond effectively and successfully to similar challenges and difficulties.

ESSENTIAL CHARACTERISTICS OF RESILIENT YOUTH

Compared to other youth, resilient youth:

- Exhibit a strong sense of self-efficacy
- Demonstrate a high level of self-confidence
- Manifest positive self-esteem and self-acceptance
- Exhibit ability to recognize and regulate emotions
- Demonstrate ability to adapt quickly to new situations
- Show the capacity to tolerate frustration and anxiety

Resilient youth show high levels of social & emotional Intelligence (SEI) as well as at least average levels of cognitive & academic intelligence (CAI), SEI is the ability to understand, manage, and express the social and emotional aspects of one's life in ways that enable the successful management of life tasks such as learning, forming relationships, solving everyday problems, and adapting to the complex demands of growth and development (Elias, Zins, Weissberg, Frey, Greenberg, Haynes, Kessler, Schwabstone, & Shriver, 1997). CAI is the ability to think critically, remember content information and to perform well on intellectual and academic tasks.

The Collaborative for Social and Emotional Intelligence (CASEL) describes Social and emotional intelligence as the ability to understand, manage, and express the social and emotional aspects of one's life in ways that enable the successful management of life tasks such as learning, forming relationships, solving everyday problems, and adapting to the complex demands of growth and development (Elias, Zins, Weissberg et al. 1997; Elias, Arnold and Hussey, 2003) noted that If IQ represents the intellectual raw material of student success, EQ is the set of social-emotional skills that enables intellect to turn into action and accomplishment. Without EQ, IQ consists more of potential than actuality. It is confined more to performance on certain kinds of tests than to expression in the many tests of everyday life in school, at home, at the workplace, in the community.

Howard Gardner's social and emotional perspective is represented in two of his eight multiple intelligences. Intrapersonal: one's capacity to form an accurate, veridical model of oneself and to be able to use that model to operate effectively in life. . . . Access to one's own feelings and the ability to discriminate among them and draw upon them to guide behavior. (Gardner, 1993; Gardner and Hatch, 1989) and Interpersonal: one's ability to understand other people: what motivates them, how they work, how to work cooperatively with them. . . . Capacities to discern and respond appropriately to the moods, temperaments, motivations, and desires of other people. (Gardner, 1993; Gardner and Hatch, 1989). Social and emotional intelligence makes a difference in the individual's life through helping the individual to experience increased Self-awareness, improvement in recognizing and naming emotions and a better understanding of the causes of feelings, a recognition of the difference between feelings and actions and better management of emotions. Students with high social and emotional intelligence, show better frustration, tolerance and anger management, fewer verbal putdowns, fights and classroom disruptions. They are better able to express anger appropriately without fighting, experience fewer suspensions and expulsions, and show less aggressive or self-destructive behavior. They demonstrate more positive feelings about self, school and family and are better handling of stress. (Goleman, 1995).

Resilient characteristics are to a large extent learned, developed, nurtured and supported by families, schools and other community support systems that provide protective factors. Several factors external to the student promote and support resilience. These include: (1) family protective factors; (2) community protective factors; (3) school protective factors. Below is a suggested model of the interactions among the three external factors and student characteristics in influencing students' achievement outcomes:

Model of Interaction Effects of School, Student and Home Factors on Youth School Performance

School Factors	Student Characteristics	Home Environment		School Performance
Strong	Strong	Strong	=	A
Strong	Strong	Weak	=	A−
Strong	Weak	Strong	=	B
Strong	Weak	Weak	=	B−
Weak	Strong	Strong	=	C
Weak	Strong	Weak	=	C−
Weak	Weak	Strong	=	D
Weak	Weak	Weak	=	F

Resilience Framework: Dynamic Reciprocal Interactions

Resilience exists in the dynamic interactions between the youth and the protective factors in the home, community and school. Youth who have developed enough social and emotional and cognitive/academic intelligence to embrace and capitalize on the protective factors that surround them are in a much stronger position to overcome risks and achieve success than those who do not have such protective factors or are unable to effectively use them.

Practical Steps to Enhance Youth Resilience

At School

- Create a positive, caring, responsive and supportive school climate
- Challenge youth to be the best that they can be
- Maintain high standards and high expectations for academic achievement and social behavior. Do not compromise standards
- Have clear rules and standards for conduct
- Increase achievement motivation and the desire to learn through engaging and meaningful learning activities in classrooms and outside of classrooms
- Provide tutoring and guidance to enhance academic achieve ment
- Help students become aware of the possibilities for a successful future.
- Provide opportunities for students to develop effective social and emotional skills such as:
  - Including and expanding Developmental Guidance activities
  - Include and expand cultural diversity and cultural awareness education
  - Provide mentoring opportunities
  - Include conflict resolution and peer mediation education
  - Include substance abuse and alcohol prevention education
  - Provide individual and group counseling
- Create a viable school management structure to support and sustain all of the above

At Home

- Read to children regularly
- Regulate television viewing
- Assign responsibilities
- Listen to concerns and help explore and develop reasonable solutions to problems
- Show interest in children's school work
- Participate in school activities including attending report card conferences
- Show interest in social activities of youth including peer relationships
- Encourage and support excellence
- Help youth think about and do what is necessary to achieve their future goals

In The Community

- Support all parents/guardians and youth particularly those who live under difficult and stressful conditions by making adequate health care available and accessible

- Provide accessible needed social services
- Provide accessible recreational programs
- Providing accessible after-school educational programs
- Support school-based programs

Partnerships

- Youth are best served when schools, families and community organizations and agencies including institutions of higher learning work together and collaborate to address their needs.
- The federally supported and funded Gear Up program is a an excellent example of a dynamic effective partnership that serves the social, emotional and cognitive/academic needs of youth, many of who are at risk and vulnerable to stressful and difficult life conditions.

The Youth

- Take advantage of the support provided in school, at home and in the community
- Seek help from responsible adults and other youth when needed
- Stay in school and do your best to achieve and succeed
- Avoid negative and high risk behaviors
- Recognize your strengths and build on them
- Recognize your weaknesses and seek help to address them
- Respect others
- Accept the fact that you are a unique person and there is no one else like you and strive to be the best you that you can be.
- Work hard
- Always do your best
- Recognize and control your emotions
- Think before you act

REFERENCES

Elias, M., Zins, J. Weissberg, R., Frey, K., Greenberg M., Haynes, N., Kessler, R., Schwabstone, M., & Shriver, T. (1997). *Promoting social and emotional learning: Guidelines for educators.* Alexandria: Association for Supervision and Curriculum Development.

Chapter Eight

Pathway Seven:
Promoting School Readiness

The relationship between school readiness and school success has long been of interest to educators and developmental psychologists. It has long been recognized that some children seem to enter school more prepared to learn and succeed than others. Children who are exposed to more positive developmental experiences are much more likely to experience school success than children who do not. The early formative years offer many opportunities as well as challenges in shaping and influencing children's later development. Recently, there has been heightened interest in and awareness of the importance of preschool readiness experiences in promoting healthy social, emotional and academic development among state and national policy makers. The new attention to school readiness from policy makers has moved the issue more center stage in our thinking about educational reform and school success for all children, especially for children in poor urban communities.

THE REAL SCHOOL READINESS QUESTION

Labeling a child "unready" for school releases the school from the responsibility of promoting that child's development. Given the potential of early childhood programs and schools to act as catalysts in the lives of children, we ask: *Are schools ready to promote development among all the children?* By rephrasing the school readiness question, we clearly indicate that it is unhelpful to label children with labels that do not directly correspond to child development.

Human development is an incremental process that spans a lifetime. While it is often helpful to talk about "stages" in children's development or "developmental milestones" that they have reached, it is far more useful when designing an intervention to ask: "Who are these particular children and what, specifically, do we need to do in order to support their development?" Child development is not a natural unfolding that ultimately culminates in a developmental milestone known as "school readiness." Whether children successfully adjust to school life depends on the quality of their *developmental experiences* during the preschool years. Developmental experiences are characterized by cognitive processing that brings psychological pleasure—a sense of well-being—that promotes future interest (Comer, 1997, private communication). Providing children with developmental experiences is a twofold process: activity + guided reflection = developmental experience. Activities by themselves are *not* developmental experiences. Thinking through or reflecting on the activity, under the guidance of an adult, is a necessary component of the developmental experience.

One of the goals set forth in the Goals 2000 education initiative states that by the year 2000, "all children will start school ready to learn." This goal statement is significant because of what it admits and what it implies. The statement admits that not all children, at present, start school ready to learn. It implies that with proper and adequate interventions, all children can begin their transition from being preschoolers to being students in schools with the prerequisite cognitive and social adaptive skills which will enable them to adapt and learn well. Many children, if given the proper preparation and opportunities and with appropriate challenges and support, can learn, achieve and succeed in school, beginning with Kindergarten.

The National Association for the Education of Young Children (NAYEC) in its position statement on school readiness in 1990 noted that: "those who are committed to promoting universal school readiness must also be committed to:

1) addressing the inequities in early life experiences so that all children have access to the opportunities which promote school success
2) recognizing and supporting individual differences among children, and
3) establishing reasonable and appropriate expectations of children's capabilities upon school entry.

Although there is general agreement that the more "ready" children are for school the more likely they are to succeed, the understanding of the concept of readiness itself has not been universally shared. There are at least three basic schools of thought about school readiness. The first perspective, the maturational view, follows in the tradition of the Gessell Institute according to which readiness is defined as biological maturation. This perspective advances the notion that maturation results in the unfolding of psycheducational and psychosocial attributes in children which make them ready or not.

The second perspective is the environmentalist perspective which places all of the emphasis on children's pre-school experiences at home and in other pre-school settings. Adult caregivers are viewed as having significant influence on children's preparedness for school by providing them with stimulating learning experiences and by creating environments that are challenging and supportive. This view notes that some children may come to school unprepared to learn due to a lack of strong developmental experiences the school's responsibility is to remedy these deficiencies. The third perspective views readiness as a combination of both maturational and environmental factors. This view was articulated by Ausubel (1963) who noted that: "readiness is a function of both general cognition maturity and particularized learning experience" (p. 30)

A number of factors influence school success for all children and especially for children from lower socioeconomic backgrounds. These factors include a school climate that is responsive to the needs of children, access to basic health care, economic security for the family, support networks to address the emotional and developmental needs of children and their families. NAYEC deems it a public responsibility to ensure that:

> " all families have access to the services and support needed to provide the strong relationships and rich experiences that prepare children to succeed in school. At a minimum such services include basic health care, including prenatal care and childhood communications; economic security, basic nutrition, adequate housing family support services; and high-quality early childhood programs" (p. 2)

QUALITY DAYCARE AND PRESCHOOL EXPERIENCES ARE CRITICAL READINESS FACTORS

In their seminal work on day care, Zigler and Gordon (1982) noted that: "By far, the thorniest issue in day care, however, is the fundamental issue of quality versus cost. While research indicates that quality makes a difference, most parents can neither afford to stay home to deliver this care themselves nor can they earn enough to purchase quality care if they work.' (p. vii). Today, access to affordable and quality child care for millions of American families continues to be a serious problem and a major local, state and national policy challenge. It is estimated that each day 13 million children are placed in day care settings yet there are major concerns expressed regarding the quality of the care these children receive (Barnett, 1995; Fosberg, 1981).

During a speech at the White House summit on child care last October, President Clinton referred to the child care problem as a "silent crisis". The critical need for child care is underscored by the fact that increasingly, in the majority of families with young children both parents work outside of the home. A recent study by Kids Count (1998) indicates that 64% of all children under 6 have both parents who work outside of the home. It is projected by the year 2000, 70% of all women with pre-school children will be working outside of the home further increasing the need for reliable affordable child care. Suzanne Martinez, director of programs and policy for the Children's Defense Fund noted: "child care is clearly the most important issue on the horizon. The cost is so high, and the quality as abysmal in places. There's going to be increasing demands for it and it's going to get more attention." New Have Register, Sunday May 24, 1998, (page A7)

Kagan and Cohen (1997) noted that although there has been an increase in day care and early educational opportunities, the demand for these services is exceeding the demand by so much that only the more affluent are being able to afford quality care thus creating serious "inequalities in access, availability and efficient distribution of services." (p. 2). The authors observed that the children who are most negatively affected by the stresses in the child care system are poor children who constitute at least 25% of all young children. Poor families have the greatest need for quality child care and early educational opportunities. They stand to benefit the most, yet they have the least access to quality services. The following statistics clearly show the need for and importance of early childhood experiences for children:

- children from low-income families are the least likely to attend early care and education programs: only percent of children living in households with incomes of $10,000 or less regularly attend early care and education programs, compared to over 75 percent of children in households with incomes in excess of $75,000 (American Academy of Pediatrics, 1996)
- Government subsidies allow some children from low-income families to enroll in early care and education programs, but funds are limited and do not allow eligible families to secure care for their children. Only small percentages of eligible low-income receive government assistance in paying for early care and education (National Association of Child Care Resource and Referral Agencies, 1996)
- Most children from low-income homes who are enrolled in preschool-59 percent- attend programs that are unlikely to provide the full range of child development, health, and parent services needed to support their school readiness.(Kamerman, 1989)
- Working-class and lower-middle-income families are also likely to rely on inadequate care. (Cohen, 1992)

The call for more pre-school programs and early child care opportunities for poor children is premised on the belief and documented evidence that many such programs and opportunities do make a substantial difference for poor children in building and enhancing their cognitive, social and psychological skills and in getting them ready for school and preparing them for successful experiences throughout their development. In the section that follows we present a review of some preschool programs and their impact on the development and lives of poor children and their families.

THE IMPACT OF PRESCHOOL PROGRAMS FOR POOR CHILDREN

Some of the strongest evidence of the potential impact of preschool services for poor children was obtained by the Cornell Consortium of Longitudinal Studies (Consortium for Longitudinal Studies, 1983; Lazar, Darlington, Murray, Royce, & Snipper, 1982). Earlier research on the effects of preschool programs focused almost exclusively on their ability to alter children's IQ scores. The findings from the Cornell Consortium was a timely response to criticism that the effects of preschool programs on children's cognitive abilities tended to "fade-out" after about three years post-intervention. (Zigler & Muenchow, 1992).

The Cornell Consortium pooled the data from eleven studies of the impact of preschool programs throughout America for disadvantaged children. These now well-known findings showed that children who attended high quality preschool programs were significantly less likely to have been retained in grade (13% of preschool participants; 31% for controls) or to have ever needed special education services for any reason (32% of preschool participants; 47% for controls). Participants (65%) were also more likely than controls (52%) to have eventually graduated from high school, though this result was not robust across all consortium studies. Additionally, standardized reading test scores showed improvement through third grade and math scores through fifth grade. Interestingly, these positive impacts persisted regardless of any "fade-out" of effects on children's IQ. The results of the Cornell Consortium accomplished much in terms of providing convincing evidence of the ability for high-quality preschool programs to positively impact the school performance of children from low-income and minority backgrounds, as well as focusing subsequent research on variables of more relevance than simple IQ scores. Studies of several individual programs, as described below, have documented the ability of preschool programs to have a positive impact on the school performance of children from low-income and minority backgrounds.

RESULTS OF MODEL PRESCHOOL PROGRAMS

Several studies have provided convincing evidence of the ability for soundly-designed and well-implemented preschool programs to improve school readiness and subsequent school performance of low-income and minority children. These studies, however, were typically conducted on programs that were implemented under ideal conditions, often with large amounts of resources and skilled personnel (Zigler & Hall, 1987). Their results, therefore, should be viewed as high-end estimates of the possible impacts of preschool services.

The Chicago Child and Parent Centers Project (Fuerst & Fuerst, 1993) documented a significant impact on participants' high school graduation rates and standardized reading and math scores in the eighth grade. Although the program provided meaningful benefits for all participants, the effects for girls was clearly more stable while the effects for boys appeared to weaken over time. These results seemed to suggest that these boys from a low-income inner-city environment faced considerably more challenges, eventually chipping away their early benefits from the Chicago Project.

Differential effects between boys and girls was even more pronounced in the results of the Syracuse University Family Development Research Program (Honig, 1977; Honig & Lally, 1982). The Syracuse Program was designed specifically for low-income preschoolers and their parents. 108 predominantly African-American families participated in the program. Results indicated that 10 years post-intervention, female, but not male, participants were less likely than controls to have been retained in grade, possessed better grades and attendance records, and were rated by their teachers as better behaved.

Like the above studies, the Houston Parent-Child Development Center Project (Walker & Johnson, 1988) focused on children and families from low-income backgrounds. In contrast, however, the Houston Project participants were predominantly Mexican-American. Also, the Houston Project served children three years old and younger, differing from most "preschool" programs. Although the Houston Project failed to show differences between groups in terms of grade retention, standardized school achievement scores were significantly higher from program attendees, relative to random-assigned controls. The impact of the Houston Project seemed to focus on improved English skills, as improvements were specific to tests that measure children's reading and vocabulary skills. Since these skills have been consistently linked to subsequent school performance, this result, though specific, is hardly trivial.

Questions regarding the relative importance of intervening early versus the importance of appropriate follow-through were first addressed by the Carolina Abecedarian Project (Campbell & Ramey, 1995; Ramey & Campbell,

1991). The Abecedarian Project supports the importance of both intervening early and providing appropriate follow-through services in order to sustain effects. In that study, 93 children were randomly divided into four groups: children who received a preschool intervention program from birth to 5 years old, children who received an elementary intervention program from 5 to 8 years old, children who received both preschool and elementary intervention programs from birth to 8 years old, and children who received no intervention services. Overall, results indicated significant positive effects of preschool participation, with no signs of effects fading out, as measured by IQ, reading and math achievement, and grade retention. There was no significant effect of the elementary intervention on IQ, both alone and in conjunction with preschool intervention. More specifically, results indicated a hierarchical order of scores in both reading and math favoring intervention that was both early and long-term. Furthermore, only 16% of children receiving both preschool and elementary interventions were retained in grade, compared to 29% who received preschool intervention only, 38% who received elementary intervention only, and 50% who received no intervention.

Clearly, High/Scope Perry Preschool Project is the strongest and most publicized example of the potential impact of a high-quality preschool program to effect long-term improvements in the lives of disadvantaged children. The results of the High/Scope Perry Preschool Study indicated many lasting benefits of early intervention for at-risk children from low-income families (Schweinhart, Barnes, & Weikart, 1993). Although IQ gains seemed to fade over time, other more important impacts showed remarkable stability, lasting well into adulthood. Follow-up at 19 years, showed that participants, relative to controls, were more likely to have graduated high school, attend college, and hold employment (Schweinhart, Berrueta-Clement, Barnett, Epstein, & Weikart, 1985). At a 27–year follow-up evaluation of the Perry Preschool Project, several more statistically significant findings were noted. Relative to controls, participants were 56% less likely to have needed special education services in school and 31% more likely to have graduated high school or to have earned a GED. Furthermore, their monthly earnings were 59% greater than controls, they were 26% less likely to rely on social services, and they were astonishingly 80% less likely to have ever been arrested. Obviously, these results are substantial and provide a considerable savings to society. The cost-benefit analysis of these results was impressive. Results indicated that the total program costs per child compared to the savings benefits (from reduced costs of social service assistance, special education, criminal losses and incarceration and from increased taxes on personal earnings) resulted in a $7.16 public return on every dollar spent on this early intervention, adjusting for inflation (Schweinhart, Barnes, & Weikart, 1993).

Positive results, such as presented above, are not alone in the literature (Schorr, 1991). Many other early intervention studies have shown remarkable benefits, such as the Milwaukee Project (Garber, 1988) which documented a 26 point IQ advantage for treated children over controls at age 5; the Harlem Project (Deutsch, 1985) whose participants at age 21 were 200% more likely to be employed, 33% more likely to have a high school diploma or GED, and 30% more likely to have post-high school education or training when compared to random controls; and the Yale University Child Study Center Project (Trickett, Apfel, Rosenbaum, & Zigler, 1981) whose participants had a 28% chance of having a serious school problem compared to a 69% chance for comparison children. These studies provide further support for the long-term efficacy of early intervention for at-risk children.

RESULTS OF LARGE-SCALE PRESCHOOL PROGRAMS

As previously mentioned, results of the above studies are particular to relatively small programs implemented under near optimal conditions. As such, they do not necessarily represent what can be expected from larger-scale programs directed at serving a national or state-wide population of children. For the most part, such programs fall under one of two groups: Head Start, a national comprehensive program serving children and families below the poverty level; or state-funded pre-kindergarten programs, a heterogeneous group of programs administered by individual states usually as an effort to improve the school readiness of poor children. Some representative research on the school readiness impacts of both of these programs are described below.

In a large meta-analysis of the Head Start research, McKey, Condelli, Granson, Barrett, McConkey, et al. (1985) showed that Head Start produced significant and quite meaningful impacts of participants' school readiness and academic achievement test results at school entry, with effect sizes in the .30's and .50's. These initial impacts, though, appeared to fade-out after three years in the public schools. Subsequent school quality may be to blame for these "fade-outs," since Head Start children typically attend elementary schools of poorer quality and are not likely to have been provided high quality transitional services (Currie & Thomas, 1997; Lee & Loeb, 1995).

More recently, results of a large national study of nearly 5,000 children (Currie & Thomas, 1995) indicated that Head Start participants, as compared to their siblings that did not attend Head Start, scored significantly higher on a measure of receptive vocabulary following Head Start participation. Head Start participation was also associated with a reduced likelihood for grade retention during elementary school. This last finding, however, was specific to

White children and was not found for African-Americans. Further research is needed to determine whether these differential results are due to characteristics of the children's backgrounds, characteristics of the schools that they attend after Head Start, or some combination of the two.

In relative contrast to Head Start, state-supported preschool programs for poor children represent a heterogeneous group of services that often differ greatly in terms of eligibility criteria and service length and intensity (National Conference of State Legislators, 1997). These programs vary considerably from state to state, both in terms of quality and the amount of financial resources allocated. The amount of money allocated to these programs seems to be independent of individual state's financial resources or region of America, indicating that their commitment may be more related to their "will" than to their "wallet" (Children's Defense Fund, 1996).

Some state-funded pre-kindergarten programs have been shown to be effective. In Georgia, a randomly-selected sample of 317 Georgia Prekindergarten Program participants were compared to eligible non-attendees (Pilcher & Kaufman-McMurrain, 1995, 1996). In kindergarten, participants were rated significantly higher than comparisons by their teachers in terms of their academic performance, communication skills, physical development, self-help skills, and social competence. Additionally, they averaged significantly fewer absences and were retained in their kindergarten year significantly fewer times (4.5% for participants versus 9.4% for comparisons). In first grade, teachers continued to rate participants as being significantly higher in academic skills. Additionally participants showed higher attendance rates and scored higher on standardized tests of both math and reading.

Georgia is not alone. Similar results were found for 351 pre-kindergarten participants as compared to eligible non-attendees in the evaluation of the Michigan School-Readiness Program (High/Scope Educational Research Foundation, 1997). In the Michigan program participants outperformed comparison children on both teacher-rating and observational measures of development in kindergarten. Comparable positive findings have also been reported for the Kentucky Preschool Project (University of Kentucky, 1995), Texas Pre-kindergarten Program (Texas Education Agency, 1995), and the Early Childhood Education and Assistance Program (Washington State University, 1993).

Some modest conclusions can be drawn about the impact of preschool programs for disadvantaged children from the research above. First, high quality programs clearly have the potential of improving the school readiness of disadvantaged children and can often lead to remarkable long-term effects in terms of improved functioning in school, work, and life. Second, the impacts of these programs may vary for different groups of children. Therefore, more clearly needs to be known about which types of programs are effective for what type of children (Guralnick, 1997). Third, significant effects can be obtained for Large-Scale programs implemented on a national or state-wide level. Research, however, has not yet adequately addressed how schools may play a greater role in supporting the initial effects of these programs. Together, these results are quite promising and set the stage for a consideration of how schools might better sustain these impacts over time.

SUSTAINING DEVELOPMENTAL GAINS

Given our understanding of healthy child development, we find it odd that critics of Head Start and other early childhood programs talk about "fade-out" or "wash-out" effects. A headstart is not a developmental milestone that once attained remains forever part of a child's developmental profile—like the ability to read. On the other side of the equation, we often see reverse progress in children's school success. Once promising students, who arrived at the doors to our schools with a "headstart," begin to fail and continue on a downward trajectory throughout their school years. We can call this the "tent" phenomena: remove the poles that support the tent and the tent collapses.

To promote children's development and learning from preschool through high school, the Comer/Zigler (CoZi) was initiated. CoZi is the merging of the Yale Child Study Center's School Development Program and Edward Zigler's Schools of the 21st Century (21C).

The first CoZi school, Bowling Park located in Norfolk Virginia, was established in 1992. As you walk into Bowling Park, Clark Boulevard— hallways have names—to the left leads to CoZi Place where the preschool and the primary school (K–3) classrooms are located. Lockamy Lane intersects Clark Boulevard and leads to the upper grade (4–5) classrooms. To the right, guidance counselor offices and the health center is seen. Sixth and seventh grade classrooms are in an annex attached to CoZi Place. Bowling Park implemented a team approach to improving the school. Preschool teachers and the elementary and middle school teachers all work together.

Instead of wondering whether the impact of early childhood programs will "fade out" once children enter elementary school, CoZi brings early childhood programs into elementary schools—and then engages the early childhood programs and the elementary schools in a coordinated process of educational change. The school community decides which early childhood programs best fit their needs. Programs include: before- and after-school care; full-year care; parent education, an information and referral resource center that informs parents about child care, health care, and other community services. Another component is its outreach program that trains family day care providers in the neighborhood. CoZi is a team approach to improving schools. Team members include administrators, early childhood teachers, elementary school teachers, noninstructional staff members, parents, community members, psychologists, social workers, and special education resource staff. To break the tyranny of the "transition" from preschool to elementary school, and to ensure the continuity of the effects of high quality early childhood programs, the school community creates a unified learning community.

REFERENCES

American Academy of Pediatrics, Advisory Committee on Immunization Practices and American Academy of Family Physicians (1996). Recommended childhood immunizations schedule/United States. Pediatrics, 97, 143–144.

Barnett, W. S. (1995). Long-term effects of early childhood programs on cognitive and school outcomes. The future of children: Long-term outcomes of early childhood programs, 5(3), 25–50.

Campbell, F. A., & Ramey, C. T. (1995). Cognitive and school outcomes for high-risk African American students at middle adolescence: Positive effects of early intervention. *American Education Research Journal,* 743–772.

Children's Defense Fund (1996). *Who cares? State commitment to child care and early education.* Washington, DC: Author.

Cohen, N. E. (1992). Increasing the quality of family child care homes: Strategies for the 1990's. *Child & Youth Care Forum, 21*(5), 347–359.

Consortium for Longitudinal Studies (1983). *As the twig is bent: Lasting effects of preschool programs.* Hillsdale, NJ: Erlbaum.

Currie, J., & Thomas, D. (1995). Does Head Start make a difference? *The American Economic Review,* 341–364.

Currie, J. M., & Thomas, D. (1997; April). Does subsequent school quality explain differential effects of Head Start? In W. S. Barnett (Chair), *Early preschool, medical, and family support services for families with young children: What makes a difference?* Symposium conducted at the biennial meeting of the Society for Research in Child Development, Washington, DC.

Deutsch, M. (1985). *Long-term effects of early intervention: Summary of selected findings.* Reports from the Institute for Developmental Studies, New York University.

Fuerst, J. S., & Fuerst, D. (1993). Chicago experience with an early childhood program: The special case of the child parent center program. *Urban Education, 28*(1), 69–96.

Fosberg, S. (1981). Family Daycare in the United States: Summary of findings-Final report of National Day Care Home Study (vol. 1) Cambridge, MA: Abt Associates.

Note: This chapter is based, in part, on work by Haynes, Ben-Avie & Gilliam.

Garber, H. L. (1988). *The Milwaukee Project: Preventing mental retardation in children at risk.* Washington, DC: American Association on Mental Retardation.

Guralnick, M. J. (1997). Second-generation research in the field of early intervention. In M. J. Guralnick (Ed.), *The effectiveness of early intervention,* 3–20. Baltimore, MD: Brookes.

High/Scope Educational Research Foundation. (1997, September). *Early returns: First year report of the Michigan School-Readiness Program Evaluation.* Ypsilanti, MI: Author.

Honig, A. S. (1977). The Children's Center and the Family Development Research Program. In B. M. Caldwell & D. J. Stedman (Eds.), *Infant education: A guide for helping handicapped children in the first three years,* 81–99, New York: Walker.

Honig, A. S., & Lally, J. R. (1982). The Family Development Research Program: Retrospective *Early Child Development and Care, 10,* 41–62.

Kagan, S. L. and Cohen, N. E. (1997). Not by chance: *Creating an early care and education system for America's children.* New Haven: The Bush Center in Child Development and Social Policy at Yale University.

Kamerman, S. B. (1989). Child care, women, work and the family: An international overview of child care services and related policies. In Lande, J. S., Scarr, S., and Gunzenhauser (Eds) *Caring for children: Challenge to America,* 93–110.

Lazar, I., Darlington, R., Murray, H., Royce, J., & Snipper, A. (1982). Lasting effects of early education: A report from the Consortium for Longitudinal Studies. *Monographs of the Society for Research in Child Development, 47*(2–3, Serial No. 195).

Lee, V. E., & Loeb, S. (1995). Where do Head Start attendees end up? One reason why preschool effects fade out. *Educational Evaluation and Policy Analysis, 17,* 62–82.

McKey, R. H., Condelli, L., Ganson, H., Barrett, B. J., McConkey, C., & Plantz, M. C. (1985). *The impact of Head Start on children, families, and communities* (DHHS Publication No. [OHDS] 90–31193). Washington, DC: U.S. Government Printing Office.

National Conference of State Legislators. (1997). *Early childhood care and education: An investment that works* (2nd ed.). Washington, DC: Author.

National Association of Child Care Resource and Referral Agencies (1996). Creating and health linkages: The role of child care resource and referral. Washington, DC: Author.

Pilcher, L. C., & Kaufman-McMurrain, M. (1995). *The longitudinal study of Georgia's prekindergarten children and families: 1994–95.* Atlanta, GA: Georgia State University.

Pilcher, L. C., & Kaufman-McMurrain, M. (1996). *The longitudinal study of Georgia's prekindergarten children and families: 1995–96.* Atlanta, GA: Georgia State University.

Ramey, C. T., & Campbell, F. (1991). Poverty, early childhood education, and academic competence: The Abecedarian experiment. In A. C. Huston (Ed.), *Children in poverty: Child development and public policy,* 190–221. New York: Cambridge.

Schorr, L. B. (1991). Effective programs for children growing up in concentrated poverty. In A. C. Huston (Ed.), *Children in poverty: Child development and public policy*, 260–281. New York: Cambridge.

Schweinhart, L. J., Barnes, H. V., & Weikart, D. P. (1993). *Significant benefits: The High/Scope Perry Preschool Study through age 27.* (Research Monograph). Ypsilanti, MI: High/Scope Educational Research Foundation.

Schweinhart, L. J., Berrueta-Clement, J. R., Barnett, W. S., Epstein, A. S., & Weikart, D. P. (1985). Effects of the Perry Preschool Program on youths through age 19: A summary. *Topics in Early Childhood Special Education, 5*(2), 26–35.

Texas Education Agency. (1995, July). *Texas evaluation study of prekindergarten programs: Final report* (Publication No. GE5-170–02). Austin, TX: Author.

Trickett, P. K., Apfel, N. H., Rosenbaum, L. K., & Zigler, E. F. (1981). A five-year follow-up of participants in the Yale Child Welfare Research Program. In E. F. Zigler & E. W. Gordon (Eds.), *Day care: Scientific and social policy issues*, 200–222. Boston: Auburn House.

University of Kentucky. (1995). *Third party evaluation of the Kentucky Education Reform Act Preschool Programs.* Lexington, KY: University of Kentucky, College of Education and College of Human Environmental Sciences.

Walker, T., & Johnson, D. L. (1988) A follow-up evaluation of the Houston Parent-Child Development Center. Intelligence test results. *Journal of Genetic Psychology, 149*, 377–381.

Washington State University. (1993, April). *1992 ECEAP longitudinal study and annual report: An evaluation of child and family development through comprehensive preschool services.* Olympia, WA: Washington State University, Department of Community Development.

Zigler, E., & Hall, N. W. (1987). The implications of early intervention efforts for the primary prevention of juvenile delinquency. In J. Q. Wilson & G. C. Lowry (Eds.), *From children to citizens, 3*, 154–185, New York: Springer–Verlag.

Zigler, E., & Muenchow, S. (1992). *Head Start: The inside story of America's most successful educational experiment.* New York: Basic Books.

Chapter Nine

Beating the Odds:
Three Case Studies

There are several important challenges which urban educators face in seeking to address the problems of urban education, especially at the high school level. Based on their work in London secondary schools, Rutter, Maughan, Mortimore, Ouston & Smith (1988) identified ten critical aspects of the high school milieu that influence student performance. They are: 1) school values and norms, 2) expectations and standards, 3) models provided by teachers, 4) feedback, 5) consistency of school values, 6) pupil acceptance of school norms, 7) shared activities between staff and pupils, 8) pupil positive of responsibility, 9) success and achievement, 10) centra-school peer groups. These ten factors are appropriate to any discussion about how best to improve the climate of urban high schools in America's innercities. However, there are other considerations which are discussed below. These are: 1) overcoming stereotypes of the urban minority student, 2) creating a school ethos that supports strong education development, 3) investing adequately and consistently in the necessary resources, human and physical capital to provide quality education, 4) improving the quality of instruction, 5) establishing and maintaining linkages with other facets of the community.

OVERCOMING STEREOTYPES

There are pervasive stereotypes about urban minority students. They are perceived and believed by many, even those who teach them, to be unambitious, unmotivated and incapable. While there is evidence to suggest that the achievement of minority students in urban schools does not match their potential, the negative stereotypes are totally false, unfounded and damaging to present and future well being of these students.

The importance for these students to derive a good sense of academic self and to obtain feelings of self efficacy concerning positive educational outcomes cannot be ever emphasized. A full awareness of the strengths and capabilities of urban minority students can help to reduce educators' misjudgment and mislabeling of students while at the same time help educators to respond effectively to the special needs of this population.

CREATING A POSITIVE ETHOS

As a social organization, the school develops a culture of its own with norms and standards of behavior. Problems arise when conflicting norms, values and standards evolve, or are brought by subgroups in the school, and there is cultural insensitivity, discrimination and intolerance by educators. A cohesive climate, in which everyone is respected is the basis for trust, full participation and meaningful involvement. The evidence shows that a supportive, caring culturally sensitive and challenging school climate is a significant factor in the degree of school success experienced by urban students. Brookover (1986) reported that 80% of the variance in student performance could be accounted for by school variables. Pallas (1988) reported significant correlations between certain school climate measures and student achievement. Rutter et al (1976) went as far as to suggest a possible casual relationship between students' school progress and the schooling process. They noted:

"The pattern of connections (among various factors including school) is complex. It is nevertheless clear that within this network, schools have a considerable degree of choice in how they are organized and that teachers have a similar choice in their decisions on how to respond to the children they teach" (p. 81).

RESOURCES

Discussions about the effectiveness of urban high schools often fail to address the critical factor of adequate resources and consistent financial support for essential academic and social programs. As indicated earlier, comparisons are consistently made between the achievement of students in poor urban high school and those in wealthier suburban schools with similar comparison of available resources, per pupil expenditures and opportunities. Comparisons reveal that in the wealthiest school districts spend many times as much per pupil as do the poorest school districts. The National Coalition of Advocates for Children (1985) reported gross inequities in school financing between wealthy and poor schools. In Massachusetts, they reported, per pupil expenditures varies from as high $5,013 in wealthy districts to as low as 1,637 in poor districts. In Texas, the top 100 school districts spend an average of $5,500 per child compared to an average of 1,800 for the bottom 100 districts. Other studies reported as much as a $30,000 difference per classroom between classrooms in rich and poor districts.

Most poor school districts are in the innercities of Urban American where an overwhelming majority of the students are minority students, primarily black and Hispanic, from low income families. The lack of consistent funding to support very badly needed educational and social programs in urban high schools is destroying the ability of these schools to adequately prepare youth for life in the American mainstream. There are some who argue that there is no relationship between education spending and student performance. They use such indices as teacher salaries as measures of spending. While teacher salaries should be competitive and teachers must be rewarded for their diligence and hard work, high teacher salaries do not necessarily guarantee a higher quality of education. Schools need good state-of-the-art equipment to challenge students educationally, strong effective social programs to recognize and capitalize on the cultural diversity and creativity of there students, as well as to teach more adaptive, social interaction, problem solving and career development skills.

QUALITY OF INSTRUCTION

Attracting highly qualified and dedicated individuals to teaching profession is becoming increasingly difficult. The Committee for Economic Development (1987) reported that schools' ability to attract the most qualified individuals as teachers has been considerable curtailed due to competition for more lucrative funds. Another concern is the preparation that teachers receive in schools of education, particularly preparation for working with urban populations (Feistritzer 1983, Haynes 1989). In a recent conversation that this author had with student-teachers at a university in an urban setting, the student-teachers indicated receiving no pre-internship preparation for work in the urban schools where they were placed. They received no information on cultural diversity, or instructional strategies that would increase their effectiveness as urban educators.

COMMUNITY LINKAGE

Urban schools are part of a constellation of services to the children and families in their communities. The connections between students' learning in the school and their future health, economic conditions and social status have been well documented, (Schorr, 1989). Furthermore, the prospects for social mobility and the perceived payoffs of graduation from school affect students' motivation to achieve (Foster, 1990).

Establishing linkages between schools, community agencies and programs is essential to the academic development of urban students. A strong connection between the urban schools at any level, but especially at the high school level, and the network of social services available can serve to reduce the social distance between schooling and real-life existence.

The Committee for Economic Development (1985) outlined and discussed several strategies for strengthening the relationship between communities and schools. The report emphasized the role of business partnerships, and identified three key types of private sector involvement: 1) funding, 2) program involvement, 3) policy involvement (p.87). The report also mentioned vocational training and cooperative education as potentially effective strategies.

Beyond the support of business, urban high schools must become one of the major centers of community life. This would require that schools host more academic, social development and recreational activities for longer hours, evenings, and on weekends. We must adjust our thinking and redirect the investment of our resources to provide what our children need to succeed in life. Edward Zigler of Yale University developed the concept of the 21st century school which would provide pre-school services to parents and children on a daily basis, including child care. High schools of the 21st century must provide equivalent support to its students and their families. Teachers and administrators, unions, school boards and local and federal government agencies much negotiate and develop policies that are driven by genuine, unwavering concerns for students' needs.

The situation in urban America is critical, and the immediate transformation of the urban school form a limited partner to a full partner in the enterprise to save and fully develop the lives of children and youth must occur immediately. We must win the war in our innercities. We must win the war against crime, violence, homelessness, poverty, teen pregnancy, school dropout, discrimination and hopelessness that threaten and diminish the lives of children in urban America. The urban high school has been fully armed and ready to be on the winning side.

INVESTIGATING HIGH SCHOOL PERFORMANCE

This author conducted a study in a large, urban and predominantly black high school, to examine factors which might contribute to the inordinately high number of failing grades among members of the sophomore class. As part of our investigation, we examined the achievement of the entire sophomore class and on the basis of Quality Point Average (QPA) which is a form of GPA except that the difficulty level of course is assessed and computed as part of QPA, we classified students into three groups only for purpose of our investigation. High achieving (QPA$<$10), Average Achieving (10$>$QPA$>$7) and Low Achieving (QPA$<$7). The highest possible QPA was 17.

There was a total of 148 students in the sophomore class. Of these, 50 (34%) fell into the high achieving group, 50 (34%) fell into the average achieving and 48 (32%) fell into the low achieving group. We examined the differences between the three groups of students on measures of self-esteem, motivation, study behavior, attitudes toward learning self-assessment and attendance. We found that the low achieving group differed significantly from the average and high achieving groups on most of the measures but that the average and high achieving groups did not differ significantly on any of the measures. The led to the conclusion that some other school related factors might have accounted for the achievement differences between high and average achieving student.

The data indicated further that significantly more males than females were among the low achievers (38 males to 10 females, a 3.8 to 1 ratio). Conversely significantly more females were among the high achievers (33 females to 17 males, an almost 2 to 1 ratio). Upon closer examination of the data it was noted that females scored significantly higher on many of the measures though not on all of them, leading to the conclusion also that some context factors might have contributed to some of the gender differences.

PRESENT STUDY

The present study was a follow-up investigation of the academic standing of the sophomore cohort we first studied.　　I returned to the High School and collected achievement information on all 148 students who were at that time completing their senior year. On the basis of these data, we reclassified students into the three achievement categories: high, average or low achieving using the same criteria established in the original study.

RESULTS

A. Reclassification

Among the original group of 50 high achievers, ten (20%) had changed their status, two (4%) had become low achievers and eight (16%) had become average achievers. Of the ten, five each (50%) were male and female and both students who had become low achievers were female.

Among the original group of 50 average achieving students, 14 (28%) had changed to either high achievers or low achievers. Eleven (22%) had become high achievers and three (6%) had become low achievers. The new group of high achievers included five males and six females. The low achievers included two females and one male.

Among the original group of 48 low achievers, fifteen (31%) were reclassified as either average or high achievers. Ten (21%) became average achievers and five (10%) became high achievers. Of the fifteen reclassified, eleven (23%) were males and four (<7%) were females. Of those reclassified as average, eight were males and two were females. Of those reclassified as high achievers, three were males and tow were females.

B. Interviews

To determine some of the possible reasons for students' having experienced a change in achievement status in either a positive or negative direction without any specific intervention designed to influence such change, I designed interview an protocol and planned to interview some students. Due to the constraints and logistical difficulties we were unable to interview students before their final day at school. I however, obtained addresses and telephone numbers of some the students, and were able to contact three of them.

Carl (a pseudonym)

Carl, a black male was originally classified as an average achiever based on a QPA of 7.17 at the end of his sophomore year. At the end of his senior year in he was reclassified as a high achiever based on a QPA of 11.0. This student graduated from high school.

At the time of the interview this student was working. He had begun attending school at a State Technical College but discontinued. His reason for discontinuing was that he changed his mind about his career choice which was graphics communication. He said that he was in the process of changing schools.

High School Experience   Carl characterized his High School as a place of challenge, high expectations and support. He asserted that teachers were hard and that they pushed him to do his best. They also were caring and supportive. For example, in response to a question by the interviewer, Carl responded:

> They (teachers) talked to me outside of class. They would take time out on their own so I could come back if I didn't understand the work. Come back, sit down

with me one on one; show me what I was doing wrong; and how I could something better to improve my grade.

Later on in the interview the following exchanged occurred: Interviewer:
Was that (teacher support) important to you. Carl: Yes, cause I felt like some-
body did care if I passed or failed the class.

The exchange seemed to reinforce Carl's perception that teachers' interest
and commitment were significant factors in his improved academic performance at his high school.

Mona (a pseudonym)

Mona, a black female was a senior at the time of the interview. She was originally classified as a high achieving student based on a QPA of 9.67, at the
end of her sophomore year. she was reclassified as a low achiever with a QPA
of 2.60 and was at the time repeating her senior year.

At the time of the interview, this eighteen year old student had two boy
children. She had the first child during her junior year and the second child
one year later. She lived with her mother and an aunt.

Mona indicated that right after she finished school her plan was to find a
job. She stated:

> I am going to work because I have two kids to take care of and I can't be sitting
> around. I'm not saying going to school would be wasting time but I have two
> kids to take care of so I have to go and get a job.

When queried about how she supported her children and whether her children's father helped she responded:

> Yes, when he feels like it. Other than that I do everything myself and I feel good
> about it; cause I take care of my kids myself and can't nobody say I don't take
> care of my kids, cause I do.

I further investigated where Mona expected to get a job. This was her
response.

> Oh, I don't even know but like my aunt and my grandmother they all work at a
> convalescent home. They could throw in a good word for me Other than that, I
> am going to try, cause I don't want a job in McDonalds or nothing like that, later
> for that check would be gone as soon as I cash it. I got to get a real job. I was
> planning on going to Stone and become a medical assistant but I guess that
> could wait for at least year or so.

I asked Mona why she felt as confident as she did about being able to raise her two children with such little support. She responded:

It going to happen; I am going to make it happen. I have to, cause nobody else isgoing to sit around and take care of my kids. I am going to have to do it myself. So that's something I am going to have to do.

High School Experience   Mona was in fifth year at her high school. She indicated that she was still in school because she became pregnant the year before and was sick all the time. She added: "this year I came to school as much I can. All my grades are good, so I'll be graduating this month".

When asked whether she could talk to teachers or other members of staff about concerns or problems, Mona identified two teachers with whom she had a fairly good relationship but then quickly added:

Some teachers like to get all in your business so that they can go and talk about you. I ain't going to mention no names."

I queried Mona about her perception of and her liking for her school. She was generally negative in her assessments. Here is what she said:

That other school (a school where half the students were white. Mona's school is all black) has all them outside activities out of school activities for for their seniors; we are not doing anything; we have a senior field trip planned but it might be canceled because don't nobody want to get involved with it. The other school, they want to Mexico for a week. This school don't do nothing like that. The other school has fund raisers. We don't do nothing.

When asked what could be done to make school better, Mona replied:

You have to make it interesting. They just tell you to come to school, sit in your class. After that it's over with. They don't make it interesting. Like when we were freshman. We had talent shows, dances, they don't have none of that anymore; they don't have nothing; they just say go to school, learn and go home. That's it; it's no fun no more.

When I asked Mona whether her parents were involved in her schooling, she replied:

No, my mother she'll try to help but some thing she just don't understand and other than that, I do it on my own.

Mona added that her mother met with her teachers only "when something happen."

Student C

John, a black male was originally classified as a low achieving student based on a cumulative QPA of 2.75 at the end of the school year. Based on a cumulative QPA of 7.00 at the end of the school year John was reclassified as an average student.

At the time of the interview John was a senior. He had repeated his junior year. He indicated that although he was doing better overall than he did during his freshman and sophomore years, that his grade had dropped slightly in the past months. He attributed this decline to the fact that he had been shot and had to miss school. He stated:

Mine (grades) got better since my freshman and sophomore year. They dropped the last couple of months since I had got shot; so I missed a lot of school. So I have been trying to be a good boy now. But basically its been better since my freshman and sophomore years.

When I asked John what accounted for his overall academic growth, this was his response.

I felt like a fool not being the only one in my family not graduating. I had to. My mother's a teacher and everything. I think I would have insulted her by not getting my diploma and stuff like that. When asked about his having been shot, John responded: I was in a bar, you know. We started fighting and stuff like that and people started shooting and I just caught a bullet; a stray bullet but now I am considered a hoodlum since I got shot. They kicked me out of school because I got shot. They thought it was something drug related and stuff like that so I had to go into the superintendent just to get back to school and all that.

I followed up on John's experience with having been shot and wanting to come back to school. I asked:

So were you kicked out of school or did you just come right back after?

John responded:

The first time I tried to come back they told me to get out of school. I was injured. They told me I had to leave or I was going to get arrested and stuff like that, cause it was some part of their policy. Now if you get shot you are going to get kicked out of school. So I had to call my mother, we had to make appointments with the superintendent and talk to him. So then he didn't even let me back in school after a while. That was after about two weeks, two or three weeks after I got shot.

The School   I inquired about John's perception of the school environment. In response to a question about how easy it was to talk to teachers and other staff, John responded in the following way:

> I don't really talk to no teachers. I really keep it to myself, otherwise I have everybody else talking about it. They already think I a hoodlum now, since I got shot. So I don't need to talk to none of them now.

I asked John to elaborate on his relationship with teachers. He stated:

> I don't trust these teachers. I don't trust them. It's (being shot) none of their business first of all. Then as I say, they always think I am a hoodlum, so why should I talk to them. They already think bad of me already. So let them keep thinking that. I show them in the long run.

I insisted that there must be something about the school that might be positive. John conceded this point and quickly countered it. He stated:

> There's a lot that's good about the school but there's a lot that could be better.

"Like what" we asked.
He replied:

> Like just for instance, the vocation wing, that's when I just come out of my carpentry class; half of our machines are broke. I've been there all three years in the same school and I only used four machines in there and the machine shop has about 20 machines in there and only about four or five of them work. You see what I'm saying. That's making us feel a little bad because we can't get the best we can get, so I can do my best work and stuff, though, the school's alright.

I asked John what he would change about his school. He responded:

> Classes are alright, maybe if the teachers, I mean the principal wouldn't act like cops and stuff like that, that would be a lot better. They'd have more people coming to school and stuff but they act like they are the police anyhow, so a lot of guy just stopped coming. Why they, got to act like that. It was already bad enough. They were there to harass us when we, at home and stuff like that; to get harassed at school that makes a person not want to come.

John had some important things to say about graduation:

> I thought I would graduate by now. Realizing I didn't it's made me better though. It make me realize my goals that I had to get out of the school and do something with my life cause going to school was easy for me; everything was

going to easy for me. I used to be able to cut classes and no teachers would say nothing to me. I still come back and pass that class and everything like that. Then when I broke my hand I have stayed back. I missed a lot of days when I broke hand. After that I started realizing I got to go to school to get my education. Can't look like no dummy in this world. You ain't going to be able to do nothing in this world if you ain't got no high school diplomas. It's bad enough people with college diplomas. I see my brother; he has a college diploma and he's still having a hard time now and he's graduated from college. It would have been a lot harder for me not graduating from high school. So I had to go back to school.

Interpretation of Interviews   The interviews appeared to support the basic point made throughout this book concerning the important elements school contexts and experiences that must exist to sustain high student performance and encourage success. All three students some in some way commented about the stereotypes, ethos, resources, quality of instruction and external support systems available to them. All three saw these factors as having had some influence on their present status, past adjustment and future plans.

An interesting observation derived from the interviews is the fact that the three students saw the same environment differently. Carl who appeared to have had the least adjustment difficulties in school also appeared to have had the least stressful life and showed the strongest academic performance. He progressed from being an average student to being in the high achieving group. Mona who by the time she was a senior had two sons was critical of the level of caring and concern demonstrated by her teachers and expressed considerable distrust of the adults in her building. Mona's status changed from being a high achieving student to a low achieving student. John who repeated his junior year because of a gun shot wound was also bitterly critical of the adults in his school and particularly angry about what he perceived to be inferior treatment reflected in poor resources because his school was predominantly black.

I became painfully aware during the interviews of how unprepared in terms of their mastery of the English language these students were. Their grammar and syntax were quite poor, often limiting their ability to express themselves very well. Yet they were about to face the world. After five years in high school they could not use the standard form of English proficiently. I was concerned about the effect this would have on their future success.

Despite the differences in perceptions, difficulties and future goals all three students displayed and expressed a determination to become well adjusted and successful adults. They spoke of acquiring employment to support themselves and their families and of proving to themselves, to their families and to the world that they were capable and worthy people. These students in my opinion gave life to the term resilience. They were set on bouncing back from adversity if given a chance at a decent life. Mona's and John's stories in particular demonstrated survivability and strength, in the face of adversity. Their cases were representative of the lives of thousands of youths in American schools who struggle to succeed and against overwhelming odds, many of them do.

REFERENCES

Bandura, A. (1989). *Perceived self-efficacy in the exercise of personal agency*. Invited address at the annual meeting of the British Psychological Society in St. Andrew, Scotland.

Brookover, W. B. (1979). *School Social Systems and Student Achievement*. New York: Praeger Publishers.

Brookover, W. B., Paterson, A. and Thomas, S. (1969). Self-concept of ability and school achievement. *Sociology of Education, 37*(3).

Committee for Economic Development (1987) *Children in need: Investment Strategies for the educationally disadvantaged*. New York, New York.

———. (1985) *Investing in our children: Business and the public schools*. New York, New York.

Feistritzer, C. Emily (1983). *The condition of teaching: Princeton Carnegie Foundation for the Advancement of Teachry*. New York.

Foster, B. (1990). *Looking for payoff: A new schooling for African-American Inner City Youth*. Jersey City: New Mind Productions.

Garmezy, N. (1982). Foreword. In E.E. Werner and R.S Smith, *Vulnerable but invincible: A study of resilient children,* (pp. xiii-xix), New York: McGraw Hill.

Haynes, N. (1989). *Proposal to establish a consortium for urban education*. Submitted to the Rockefeller Foundation New Haven: Yale Child Study Center.

National Coalition of Advocates for Students (1985). *Barriers to excellence: Our children at risk*: Boston, MA.

Pallas, A.M. (1988) School climate in American high schools. *Teachers College Record, 89*(4), 542–554.

Rutter, M., Maughan B., Mortimore, P. Ouston, J. with Smith A. (1979). *Fifteen thousand hours*. Cambridge, MA. Harvard University Press.

Schorr, L. B. with School D. (1988). *Within our reach: Breaking the cycle of disadvantage*. New York Anchor Press, Doubleday.

Schunk, D. H. (1989). Self-efficacy perspective on achievement behavior. *Education Psychologist, 19*(2), 48–58.

Epilogue

School Success: Reflections of A Thirteen-Year-Old High School Freshman

Monique Haynes

> Education should consist of a series of enchantments, each raising the individual to a higher level of awareness, understanding, and kinship with all living things.
>
> —Unknown author

Every student in the world today has the potential to succeed. The only question is, how much time and effort are they willing to put into the process of accomplishing their aspirations? It would be a more difficult challenge to reach success if students have goals but do not work towards them and if they are not provided with the materials, support, and guidance that they need. There should be more programs after school for students such as tutoring, peer tutoring, book clubs, and other after school programs. The schools should provide councilors for every student in the school, who can aid the students and most important of all, encourage them. Schools should also try to incorporate parents into school activities as many ways as possible. Teachers should prepare lesson plans that will properly prepare students well for college, especially in the public schools. If all of these programs, challenging lessons in the class room, and parental participation take place then students will be properly equipped to reach success in the future. From there, it will be the students' responsibilities to work hard to accomplish their dreams because if they do not put forth exertion to reach their goals, then no one will put forth the effort in helping them reach their endeavors.

> Tell me and I forget; show me and I remember; involve me and I understand.
>
> —unknown

Many students truly need help with school work and homework but are too afraid to ask for extra help. They are not afraid of the teacher, but believe it or not, many high school students are afraid that their peers will find it amusing that they need a bit of extra help. The truth is the students who find seeking extra help amusing need the help more than the students who want to ask. Asking for assistance in class can be a bit embarrassing and maybe even intimidating but when one student gathers up enough courage to ask the teacher to go over a problem it turns out that the other students did not understand the problem either. Students should not be scared to ask for help in the class room but there are a few students who would prefer a one on one session. This is why there should be after school tutoring programs. After school the students can talk with teachers and receive help without feeling as if the other students will laugh and make fun. Sometimes students feel that the teacher may think less of them if they ask for help or sometimes the teachers are not available to stay after school and provide help to the students. These are problems are reason enough to have peer tutoring. Students from higher grades tutor the students in the grades beneath them and some them may even have had the same problems that the students receiving the tutoring have. This way both students feel comfortable because they are both children and can relate to each other. In the tutoring programs students can get their homework done and have time to socialize. Many students go home after school and park themselves in front of the television. The homework sits patiently in their book bags waiting to be started. The next day in class the students tell the truth and say that they did not understand the homework, and that is because they did not make an attempt to do it. Book clubs, sports clubs, music bands, and many other clubs keep students from going home and watching television and getting into trouble on the streets. Many students do not know what to do after school so they linger on the streets and eventually wind up getting into trouble. If schools provided after school activities that appeal to all students then the students will not get in trouble and will not fill their minds with the shows on television. Book clubs and book bowls get students to be interested in reading and help build their vocabulary and writing skills. Schools should provide fun activities also to get students interested and to stay after school. Perhaps there should be a rule that if students wish to join the dance group or basket ball team, they must maintain a B average. This way, students are obligated to keep their grades in top shape if they wish to join a club. Schools must try to involve students in academic activities while at the same time catering to their likes. Students often learn more if they are talked with and not at and if they are given the opportunity to hands-on activities. Involvement is one of the great keys to success and if one is not involved, he or she is depriving him or herself of great lifetime experiences.

You really can change the world if you care enough.

—Marion Wright Edelman

Counselors are important people in students' lives because they help students fill out college applications, pick out their classes, and listen to any problems the students may have. In almost every school one can find counselors, yes, but are those counselors working to their highest potential? Counselors should care about the students who come to them with questions and those who come in search of assistance. The advice counselors give should be from their hearts and what they truly believe. Counselors should tell students to work to their full aptitude. Students take to heart the advice that counselors give because counselors are supposed to look out for and guide their students. Not all counselors take the time to sit down with students and talk about colleges and career goals. Much of the time when students go to speak with their counselor, the counselor is in a meeting or is not available.

Counselors should encourage their students and advise them in the best way they know possible, as if they were advising their own children. No student deserves to be told that he or she is not good enough and no student deserves not to have someone who cares about their future endeavors. Due to this, schools should scout out the best counselors that they can find and make sure that those counselors are willing to put in the hours and answer all of the brilliant questions students have.

Counselors are not the only individuals who should be giving guidance and encouragement to students. Parents should be giving the bulk of the support and love. Children follow the examples that their parents set and put to action the advice they are given by their parents. Parents have the strongest effect on choices their children make and unfortunately many parents do not care. To keep those parents who do want their children to do well involved, schools have set up parent teacher nights, send home progress reports, notices about the activities taking place in school, and invite parents to observe their children's worth ethic and demeanor in school. Parents should take that extra step to get involved in their children's lives and the schools should provide parents with the opportunity. When children are encouraged they feel as if they can do anything they put their mind to and the truth is they can.

The mediocre teacher tells. The good teacher explains. The superior teacher demonstrates. The great teacher inspires.

—William Arthur Ward

Teachers hold students' future in their hands. If they do not teach the students well then the students will suffer from that experience. Teachers make lesson plans every day with the intention of using that lesson plan during class. If that lesson plan has the same material on it that it did the day before, the teacher is taking a step towards failing his or her students. If the lesson plan has review on it for a whole semester, the teacher takes another step towards failing his or her students. If that lesson plan has no tests or quizzes, the teacher and students step once again towards failure. If there is no homework on the lesson plan the teacher has brought his or her students a step away from failure.

If a teacher gives all of his or her students A's after all the work they did was a review, he or she has failed those students. Maybe those students did not fail that year but the next year when the students advance to the next grade or graduate and begin college, they will realize that they were failed. Those students will have to catch up to the students who had teachers who taught them and even went ahead to teach them advanced material.

Teachers should teach their students the material that they are going to need to know to advance to the next grade and to move on to college. On college the professors do not wait for everyone to understand the material and then move on. Those professors expect students all to be ready and to know certain facts. Teachers play a major role in educating children and should teach students everything they know.

> The most practical, beautiful, workable philosophy in the world won't work—
> if you won't.
>
> —Zig Ziglar

I was once asked what helped me do so well in school. I contemplated for a couple minutes and then responded "myself." Of course my family, my school, and my teachers helped me do well in school but in order for someone to do well he or she has to decide that he or she wants to do well. The person who can give you success is yourself. Family and teachers can provide all the preparation for students but they cannot take tests for students, they cannot take the SAT'S for students, and they cannot force students to want to do well. Students have to tell themselves what kind of future they would like to have because only a few people make it in the NBA and WNBA and even fewer people make it in Hollywood. The career decision does not have to made right away but the decision that one wants to succeed has to be made as soon as one is old enough to make his or her own choices.

Once that decision is made by one student then other students will look on and believe that there can be an excellent future for them and that they can make a good living. One can say that success is contagious, once one person has it everyone wants it.

"Without goals, and plans to reach them, you are like a ship that has set sail with no destination."

Fitzhugh Dodson

Schools are homes to students during the day where they learn, think, and solve every day problems. Parents trust that schools will teach their children to the highest capability and prepare them well for the future. After school programs will keep their children out of trouble and help interest students in activities they never thought they could be interested in, counselors and parents can give students all of the support, guidance, care, and love, that they will carry with them through the course of their lives, teachers can teach students the information they will need to know to advance on to college, and most important of all, students can make a promise with themselves that they will succeed no matter how difficult times can and will get.

All of this support and determination provide students with the formula to happiness and success. When the next generation is looked upon what is seen is the next generation of doctors, lawyers, and teachers. The future is seen in their faces and if schools prepare the next generation of children well, and families provide support and become involved in these children's lives, then the next generation will be ready to make all the great discoveries that lie ahead, and be ready to make their dreams of success come through.

"There are important cases in which the difference between half a heart and a whole heart makes just the difference between signal defeat and a splendid victory."

—A.H.K. Boyd

Postscript

Norrisa Haynes and Monique Haynes

We are fortunate to have had excellent teachers, counselors and other adults in our schools who have helped us to do well, not just academically but also socially and emotionally. Sometimes we may not have immediately appreciated the lessons that our teachers were attempting to teach when they criticized or chastised or demanded more from us. But now we realize that they were challenging us to be the best we could be. They believed in us and wanted us to believe in ourselves; in our ability to do well if we worked hard and set high goals for ourselves. We think that the fact the adults in our schools challenged us, not in a way that put us down and made us doubt ourselves, but in a way that showed that they accepted us and recognized what we were capable of achieving made us want to do better and made us want to meet their expectations. We felt accepted and respected by most of our teachers and other adults in our schools.

Now that I, Monique am in high school, I realize that all of the patient support and guidance I received from my teachers in elementary and middle school will help me to be a good student in high school. I have learned from them that I must study hard and become involved in other activities that would help me to be a well-rounded student and individual. The lessons I learned from them will help me to succeed.

Now that I, Norrisa, am in College, I look back over the challenging, turbulent and yet happy years of elementary, middle and high school and I thank my teachers, counselors and other adults in my schools for the gifts they have given me in the form of acceptance, believe and challenge. I had committed, dedicated and genuinely loving teachers and other adults in every school I attended. These individuals made a tremendous difference between success and failure in my life.

Of course, without our parents we would not be who we are today. Our parents expected us to succeed and made success possible through their unconditional love and support. It is very important in our view for schools and parents to work closely together to help children succeed. We both believe that the pathways to success that are discussed in this book helped us and that others too may find them helpful.

Index of Terms